# Journey to the Metaverse

# Journey to the Metaverse

*Technologies Propelling Business Opportunities*

Antonio L. Flores-Galea

BEP
BUSINESS EXPERT PRESS
*Leader in applied, concise business books*

*Journey to the Metaverse: Technologies Propelling Business Opportunities*

Cover design by Charlene Kronstedt

Interior design by Exeter Premedia Services Private Ltd., Chennai, India

First published in 2023 by
Business Expert Press, LLC
222 East 46th Street, New York, NY 10017
www.businessexpertpress.com

ISBN-13: 978-1-63742-438-4 (paperback)
ISBN-13: 978-1-63742-439-1 (e-book)

Business Expert Press Collaborative Intelligence Collection

First edition: 2023

10 9 8 7 6 5 4 3 2 1

*To Ana, who created magical moments*
*of inspiration to write this book.*

# Description

The *Metaverse* will be the next technological revolution. This book helps business executives to understand its foundations and reveals the new opportunities it will bring. The author is a renowned engineer with more than 20 years of experience who started working as a business adviser for large corporations and start-up companies around the world after graduating from his international MBA, 10 years ago.

The **accessible language** used to explain the **complex technologies** involved is key to understanding the **business opportunities** that the Metaverse will bring. The book follows a smooth but thorough journey along all aspects associated with the Metaverse, from *augmented reality, virtual reality, digital currencies,* the *Internet of things, 3D glasses,* and many others. This book contains **trustful, actionable, and practical insight** from the experience of a person highly involved in technical activities and used to speak to the board of many corporations.

On reading this book, you will understand not only the drivers behind the Metaverse but also the following milestones and the roadmap we can expect: an *early insight* to adapt your business strategy or professional career to get the most out of this new social paradigm.

## Keywords

metaverse and how it will revolutionize everything; metaverse handbook; metaverse investing; metaverse marketing; web3; metaverse; virtual and augmented reality; blockchain revolution; NFT

# Contents

# Testimonials

*"Antonio Flores-Galea explains in an accurate way virtually everything about the Metaverse from a non-technical perspective that helps anyone understand the concepts and technologies. It manages an important feat: to condense a lot of knowledge, experience, and information in a limited space. The book serves as a quick, robust guide while providing additional directions for further inquiry in all fields."*—**Stylianos Mystakidis, Innovator & Researcher, University of Patras, Greece**

*"This book makes an intuitive connection between the metaverse and the commercial world without using technical jargon."*—**Lik-Hang Lee, Assistant Professor, Korea Advanced Institute of Science & Technology (KAIST)**

# Preface

When I received my agent's call asking me to write about something appealing to many people, especially decision makers and business people worldwide, related to my expertise, my answer was clear: the Metaverse.

Having worked for more than 20 years in highly innovative fields such as computer vision, artificial intelligence (AI), broadband communications, robotics, mobile devices, and some more, the Metaverse is not just a concept or trending word to me, but the next revolution society will face. And it will be, from my point of view, the most profound transformation of humanity, far beyond the industrial revolution, the massive adoption of the automobile, electricity, or the Internet. The reason behind this affirmation is that, in the long term, there is even a risk that humans not only embrace artificiality, by building cities instead of living in caverns, having health care and diet instead of dying at 30, multiplying by billions, and still having a societal structure to make it sustainable, and so on. With the future wide adoption of the Metaverse, humans could split from nature for good, either by incorporating artificial implants in our body—or even replacing some parts to become *cyborgs*—or losing interest in the real environment and spending our lives immersed in virtual worlds that only exist as bits inside mega-computational nodes.

This book tries to explain *everything* about the Metaverse from a non-technical perspective, so anyone can understand the concepts and technologies that will hold up the Metaverse from a high-level point of view. Although there is a lot of news speaking of the Metaverse, I believe the *information* is scattered and frequently hidden behind marketing messages, mostly because this appealing concept is being used by many companies to speak about nearly anything, even if it is not related to the Metaverse at all.

Before starting to describe anything about the Metaverse, let me explain why you will find the word written capitalized or not in different parts: the same way we refer to *the* Internet (with capitalized "I") as the global network that connects all our devices and *an* internet (with small initial) as a network that operates the same protocols but at a limited scale (e.g., when saying "the Chinese internet"), we refer to the Metaverse (capitalized "M") in this book as the global immersive infrastructure and service jointly provided by all players, while we speak of a metaverse (with small initial) when referring to a local or limited solution developed by a company that is not necessarily connected to the rest (as, for instance, when saying "Meta is developing its own metaverse").

That said, when speaking of the Metaverse, the first thing to consider is that its underlying technologies are not new at all. In fact, when I speak about the Metaverse, my time as a university professor comes to mind. And I see a complete equivalence between the Metaverse and AI. In the late 1990s, AI was mostly developed at a theoretical level. I studied and taught about the technologies underlying AI: neural networks, Kohonen maps, expert systems, chaos theory, computer vision algorithms, and so on. Everything that makes AI a reality today was there, in books, two decades ago and, sometimes, even before. There were two problems that took so long to solve: first, huge computational power was needed to make those algorithms practical—nobody would wait for a GPS to take two hours to calculate a route considering traffic, for instance—and second, digitalizing the world was needed—AI needs digital (or digitized) data and digital devices. Now we have plenty of digitized data and affordable digital devices that are millions of times more powerful than those in the 1990s.

The Metaverse will follow the same maturity cycle: the theory is there, even some experimental devices and applications, but we need far more computing power, network bandwidth, and digitization. However, everything moves faster with time and much less than two decades will surely be needed to see the true Metaverse in action. And we must be prepared for that moment because the Metaverse will transform business, social relations, leisure, homes, offices, streets, and the law. Such a profound change will take some time to happen at its entire scale, but early adopters will enjoy some advantages and will be much better prepared not only to make more profit or get a better job but also to enjoy a better quality of life.

This book intends to be a guide for these early adopters, or at least to illustrate what is there and let you make your decision regarding the

Metaverse era: *when* to start and *how* to start. It is not a recipe book, so you will not find any "to-do list" or a similar one here. To-do lists are valid for deterministic tasks (assembling furniture, replacing your car's battery, enrolling in college …) but the evolution of the Metaverse still presents a lot of uncertainties, so the best way to address this is through critical thinking. And for critical thinking, the only thing needed is knowledge. So, this book aims at giving you the knowledge you will need to make your best decisions.

You will find first some concepts and general explanations about the Metaverse and a bit of history, in Chapters 1 and 2. Chapter 3 is about the implications of the Metaverse in different industries. Chapter 4 shows what companies are currently investing large sums in developing their Metaverse applications, services, or devices. After these introductory chapters, you will find descriptions of the Metaverse underlying technologies described from Chapter 5 to Chapter 9. Chapters 10, 11, and 12 show the current state of the art regarding the Metaverse, the immediately expected evolutions, and some examples that we can already find in the market. The final part of the book, from Chapter 13 to 17, covers some questions that may arise after reading the previous chapters regarding potential security and privacy issues, technological challenges that the Metaverse adoption represents, possible side effects, and what else can we expect once the Metaverse turns into reality. Finally, Chapter 17 is about some personal recommendations in the short term.

I hope you enjoy the reading and I also hope we can meet someday … maybe inside the Metaverse.

# Acknowledgments

I want to thank all people who helped me make this venture a reality. First, to my agent Nigel Wyatt, who made me find the best route to communicate my experience and knowledge about the Metaverse and its underlying technologies to you.

I want also to thank all the experts and professionals who shared discussions with me about some aspects of this book, especially Lik-Hang Lee (Paul), professor of Metaverse-related subjects in KAIST, the Korea Advanced Institute of Science and Technology; Tony Parisi, the father of the "Seven Rules of the Metaverse" and an active entrepreneur, now leading the strategy of the promising Laminal project; and Stylianos Mystakidis, the writer of the Metaverse entry in Encyclopedia.

Finally, I want to thank my wife Ana for her ideas, support, and encouragement to make the writing of this book much more thrilling and amusing. Some important elements and ideas around the book in your hands were ideated by her.

# CHAPTER 1

# What Is the Metaverse?

The Metaverse, as a concept, is not new. It first appeared in Neal Stephenson's science fiction novel *Snow Crash* published in 1992, representing a parallel virtual reality (VR) universe, created from computer graphics, that users from around the world could access and connect through glasses and earphones. The backbone of that *metaverse* was a protocol called "street," which linked different virtual neighborhoods and locations. Users "materialized" in the Metaverse in configurable digital bodies were called "avatars." A relevant cue in Stevenson's novel is that digital experiences in the Metaverse could have a real impact on physical users' bodies.

In the scientific arena, the first publication about the Metaverse was published on the *Web of Science* six years later in 1998. However, the Metaverse concept, although having existed for a long time and has been widely used in mass media lately, is still under construction and in constant evolution. This is because it relies on developing technologies, much likely to what happened to the "Internet" concept two decades ago.

In plain language, the Metaverse relates to the "hyper-spatiotemporality" concept, building a virtual world parallel to the real world. It breaks the boundaries of time and space and offers users an open, free, and immersive experience. We can imagine the Metaverse as a 3D worldwide web (WWW) where users navigate between artificial environments and objects and see virtual representations (faithful or fake) of other users, called ***avatars***. However, the Metaverse does not end there; the digital 3D spaces—***virtual worlds***—will have **physical connections with the real world** (e.g., simulating the weather in real time, showing the meeting room of an office with the physical attendants as a virtual copy in the virtual world, etc.).

If we want a formal definition for the Metaverse, Stylianos Mystakidis's entry in Encyclopedia describes the Metaverse as (Mystakidis 2022):

*The post-reality universe, a perpetual and persistent multiuser environment merging physical reality with digital virtuality. It is based on the convergence of technologies that enable multisensory interactions with virtual environments, digital objects, and people such as virtual reality (VR) and augmented reality (AR). Hence, the Metaverse is an interconnected web of social, networked immersive environments in persistent multiuser platforms. It enables seamless embodied user communication in real-time and dynamic interactions with digital artifacts. Its first iteration was a web of virtual worlds where avatars were able to teleport among them. The contemporary iteration of the Metaverse features social, immersive VR platforms compatible with massive-multiplayer online video games, open game worlds, and AR collaborative spaces.*

Some important concepts, which will be analyzed throughout this book, arise in this definition:

- **Multiuser, social, real-time dynamic interaction**: We will analyze how the essence of the Metaverse is to work as the next generation of social relationships at a large scale, the new opportunities this will bring to the table, and the risks.
- **Merge between physical reality and digital virtuality, multisensory interactions, and immersive environments**: We will see how further technological advancement, new complex devices, sensors, and networks are still needed to produce a practical, democratized Metaverse.
- **VR and AR**: Both concepts are related to digital environments that can expand, change, or even substitute the aspect of the perceived reality by someone. In this book, we describe how this is achieved and what other less popular technologies are related to this *enabler* of the Metaverse.
- **Avatars, teleport, and video games**: These concepts, among some others, are frequently dropped in many articles related to the Metaverse, so they will also be analyzed and clarified in this book.

## The Evolution of the Internet

Some authors describe the Metaverse as a collection of 3D virtual worlds connected with each other via the Internet (Dionisio and Gilbert 2013), or a new type of Internet application and social form that integrates a variety of new technologies. Although true, I believe this is an incomplete definition because the Internet is the *primitive* technology that supports the Metaverse: the Metaverse would never be born without the Internet, but the Internet will be soon perceived as a basic, simple technology that enables the Metaverse. It is very similar to the case of the combustion engine and cars: the car would never be born without a combustion engine, but nowadays electric cars make combustion engines an obsolete technology. In the same way, once the Metaverse is fully deployed and mature, surfing the Internet or posting on social media will much likely disappear.

This is because the Metaverse represents a such impressive improvement in the state of the art of social communication and information sharing that people will move from the "2D world," based on "scroll and click," to the "3D world," based on feeling and acting as we do in our real life; something very similar to the shift from phone calls to instant messaging that happened between 2010 and 2020.

As the natural evolution of the Internet, the Metaverse provides an immersive experience based on AR technology, creates a **mirror image** of the real world based on **digital twin** technology, builds an **economic system** based on **Blockchain** technology (e.g., using cryptocurrencies), and tightly *integrates* the virtual world and the real world into the economic system, the social system, and the identity system, allowing each user to produce content and *edit* the world. Unlike the real world, where each of us has limitations, the Metaverse, by its own conception, brings much more freedom, flexibility, and power—at least in theory.

However, as already mentioned, the Metaverse is a concept that is constantly evolving, and different participants are enriching its meaning in their own ways. Thus, the theoretical model and the practical result may differ, like what happened to the "freedom of speech" promised by the Internet open architecture and the discretional censorship practiced by several social platforms at present. We will further discuss the ethical implications and the risks associated with the Metaverse in the later chapters of this book.

## The First *Iteration* of the Metaverse—the Web 3.0

As the Metaverse is evolving very fast, the scientific community has agreed to speak about different *iterations* of the Metaverse, referring to subsequent redefinitions of the concept, adding more features, or adapting the previous conception.

When VR technology was gaining traction, the Metaverse was considered the "3D Internet," also called **Web 3.0** or "**Web3**." As shown in Figure 1.1, this name was given as the third evolutive step of the Internet, being Web 1.0 the original static version of the WWW, and Web 2.0 mostly dominated by social media and multimedia content sharing. Web 3.0, although not exactly matching the Metaverse concept, is considered the ignition of the Metaverse enabling technologies such as VR, Blockchain, artificial intelligence (AI), and more.

But, even before Web3 technologies were generalized, the Metaverse already started to use them in early and mostly experimental ventures. It was conceived as a web of virtual worlds where avatars would be able to travel seamlessly among them. Under that definition, the first metaverse was CitySpace, which was only active from 1993 to 1996. Subsequently, different social and standalone metaverses—virtual worlds—such as Active Worlds and There (www.there.com) emerged. Some more ambitious initiatives regarding the achievement of interconnected spaces arose, like the open-source software "OpenSimulator," which was—and still is—reachable through a network created in 2010, called "Hypergrid." This

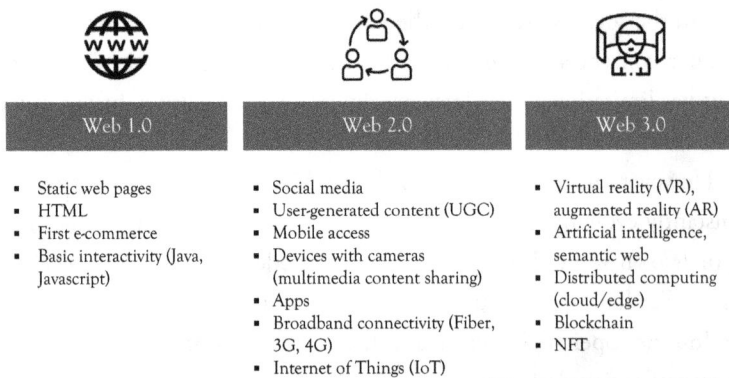

| Web 1.0 | Web 2.0 | Web 3.0 |
|---|---|---|
| • Static web pages | • Social media | • Virtual reality (VR), augmented reality (AR) |
| • HTML | • User-generated content (UGC) | • Artificial intelligence, semantic web |
| • First e-commerce | • Mobile access | |
| • Basic interactivity (Java, Javascript) | • Devices with cameras (multimedia content sharing) | • Distributed computing (cloud/edge) |
| | • Apps | • Blockchain |
| | • Broadband connectivity (Fiber, 3G, 4G) | • NFT |
| | • Internet of Things (IoT) | |

*Figure 1.1 The major evolutions of the Internet and their supporting technologies*

network allows the movement of digital agents and their inventory across different platforms through hyperlinks. Although aiming to become a truly interconnected open and virtual world, Hypergrid always remained as an experiment and never became compatible with proprietary virtual worlds such as the popular Second Life (www.secondlife.com), developed by Linden Lab in 2003.

## The Second Iteration—Multigaming

Currently, the second iteration of the Metaverse is under construction where social, immersive VR platforms will be compatible with massive-multiplayer online video games, open game worlds, and AR collaborative spaces. According to this vision, users can meet, socialize, and interact without restrictions in an embodied form as 3D holograms or avatars in physical or virtual spaces.

In the Metaverse, an **avatar** means an alter ego used as the virtual identity of a user in the different virtual worlds. Initially, avatars were mostly used as an exaggerated form in the virtual world rather than reflecting the actual user aspect or his ideal ego and were especially used in gaming. Over time, they gradually evolved into an ideal form that projects the outward appearance and reflects the ego. An avatar performs a social role and social interaction in the Metaverse. In the Metaverse, avatars are expected to be highly configurable, including not only physical features but also costumes and items, used as a medium to express the users' social meaning. In fact, various luxury clothing companies are paying attention to selling virtual items in the Metaverse to serve that purpose. It is important because, even today, younger generations consider their profile meaning in social media as important as their physical appearance, as they think that their identities in virtual spaces and reality are the same.

Regarding users' social interaction at present, it is possible with several limitations, mainly because everything must be done within the same platform. Cross-platform and cross-technology meetings and interactions, where some users are in VR and others in AR environments, are the next frontiers. Common principles of the Metaverse include software interconnection and user "teleportation" between worlds. This requires the interoperability of avatar customization and the portability of accessories, properties, and inventory, based on common standards.

If we go to tangible commercial applications, two games are considered the ground for practical metaverses: Roblox, released in 2006, and Minecraft, by the Swedish company Mojan Studios, in 2009. However, it was not until March 2021 when Roblox included the concept of "metaverse" in its prospectus for the first time, probably to better land on the New York Stock Exchange. The company's market value exceeded $40 billion on its first day of listing, and the "Metaverse" concept started to become a famous word. Thus, 2021 can be declared as the first year of existence of the practical Metaverse, although it must be considered just a very limited version of what is yet to come.

In fact, we are still far from having a true Metaverse. In the current development phase, the Metaverse has integrated 5G, cloud computing, computer vision, Blockchain, AI, and other cutting-edge science. Nevertheless, as we will see next, more evolution is still needed to make the Metaverse suitable and attractive for daily activities and commercial digital services.

## The Next Iteration—the True Metaverse

Once the supporting technologies of the Metaverse—AI, interactive technologies, cloud computing, and edge computing—are mature enough, the true potential of the Metaverse will come to our lives progressively, with much more improved accuracy of vision and language recognition, and the development of generative models that enable more immersive environments and natural movements. The true Metaverse will neither rely on computers nor even smartphones or tablets. It will leverage the large bandwidth provided by 5G and 6G mobile networks and the proliferation of smart city services and wearable sensors and devices to expand our interaction dramatically. The Metaverse will "invade" all social aspects, such as fashion, events, games, education, and work, based on immersive interaction and services natively designed in the Metaverse. A comparison of such a paradigm shift can be made, for example, with the appearance of movies to tell stories as an evolution of books when the cinematographic technology was born.

This will be achieved progressively over time, and nobody foresees the true Metaverse coming in the short term. The Internet needed some decades to mature, and something similar is expected about the Metaverse. You will find the pillars to *predict* the future of the Metaverse in this book, but you need to digest the concepts in a realistic way and realize that innovations and disruption will come along different stages. This book is an insight to let you be ahead of the common knowledge about this matter.

Under these premises, and expecting scattered and isolated initiatives in this early stage, author Tony Parisi has postulated **the seven rules of the Metaverse** as a high-level manifesto, a proposal for future development based on previously accumulated experience with the development of the Internet and the World Wide Web (Table 1.1).

According to his proposal, there should be only **one Metaverse** (rule #1), it should be **for everyone,** (#2) **open** (#4), **hardware-agnostic** (#5), **networked** (#6), and **collectively controlled** (#3). Speaking with Parisi, he does not see the seven rules as instructions that need to be implemented but as a set of characteristics that the Metaverse must have to achieve scale and be resilient enough to survive in the long term. According to him, the Metaverse must be "interconnected, serving a broad set of use cases, controlled by no single entity, based on open standards, running on the widest range of hardware devices, powered by a heterogeneous network of computers communicating with each other, and forming the fabric of the future Internet." I agree that this is inevitable for the Metaverse to become mainstream because technical achievements and socioeconomic forces will drive it in this direction.

Table 1.1 *The seven rules of the Metaverse (Tony Parisi)*

| #1 | There is only one Metaverse. |
|----|------------------------------|
| #2 | The Metaverse is for everyone. |
| #3 | Nobody controls the Metaverse. |
| #4 | The Metaverse is open. |
| #5 | The Metaverse is hardware independent. |
| #6 | The Metaverse is a Network. |
| #7 | The Metaverse is the Internet. |

However, although this is the final vision of a mature Metaverse, we will expect some more or less isolated initiatives first and a look for standardization and convergence as the Metaverse grows in users and applications, very much like what happened to other technological revolutions in the past. According to Parisi, there are core technologies that still need to be developed, standards that must be defined, and use cases and usage patterns that will be established by the early generations of Metaverse content creators. An interesting question about the governance of the Metaverse is related to whether there will be new standards organizations and even new authorities beyond current geographical schemes (countries), which are currently struggling to regulate global phenomena like cryptocurrencies, social media, and the Internet itself, or the ecosystem will remain more or less the same. The latter means the ecosystem would be based on decentralized or centralized governance and accountability for the different virtual spaces in the Metaverse, and other areas related to it, which will be explained in Chapter 13. But, before that, in the following chapters of this book, we will discover how the Metaverse is being developed, what industries are or should be interested in placing services and assets in the Metaverse, and what building technologies will enable the successful global implementation of the Metaverse.

## Summary

In this chapter, we have read about the following ideas:

- The Metaverse is a concept to describe the next digital revolution, the evolution of the Internet to be immersive, collaborative, social, and fully blended with the physical world.
- Three *iterations* are considered in the history of the Metaverse since its conceptual description in 1992: the "Web 3.0," the "multigaming integration," and the "true Metaverse."
- We are now in the "Web 3.0" iteration, where developments mainly consist of adaptations and extensions to the current Internet (adding virtual reality—VR, cryptocurrency payments, isolated social VR games …).

- The second iteration will bring interoperability between games and applications, letting us enjoy a single avatar or "virtual entity" of us in the Metaverse. Our avatar will become "a part of us."
- The third iteration will bring the true Metaverse as mainstream, moving a big share of our daily activities to the virtual world. This still requires a lot more computing power than what is available today, many new devices (wearables, AR contact lenses, etc.), and the development of new services and applications in a society where the access to the Metaverse is generalized.

# CHAPTER 2

# Is the Metaverse for Video Gaming?

Video game technology is the most intuitive way of presenting the Metaverse. It can not only provide a creative platform for the Metaverse but also realize the aggregation of interactive content and social scenes. Mobile game publishers have shown the most interest in joining the Metaverse early, as shown in Figure 2.1, representing 19 percent of apps with "Metaverse" as a keyword in their title or description. Furthermore, most of the apps in the category of social and entertainment can be also considered games.

A game engine is the core of any video game technology. It refers to the core components used as a common basis to develop computer games or some real-time interactive image applications that provide responsive graphical environments in games. The appearance of game engines reduced the difficulty for game designers and developers to develop new games as they do not need to be coded from scratch. The development of game engines drives the development of 3D images and environments in the Metaverse and provides users with an experience closer to the real world.

## Playing in the Metaverse Before It Exists

This is probably the most potent reason why, whenever we see an example of Metaverse applications, we see a gaming avatar moving inside a 3D scene, precisely like in games. In fact, in the game world, the examples of metaverses—understood under the restrictive definition of virtual worlds—such as Roblox (www.roblox.com), Sandbox (www.sandbox .game), Fortnite (www.epicgames.com/fortnite) are increasing day by day. A current competitive landscape of vendors providing solutions for

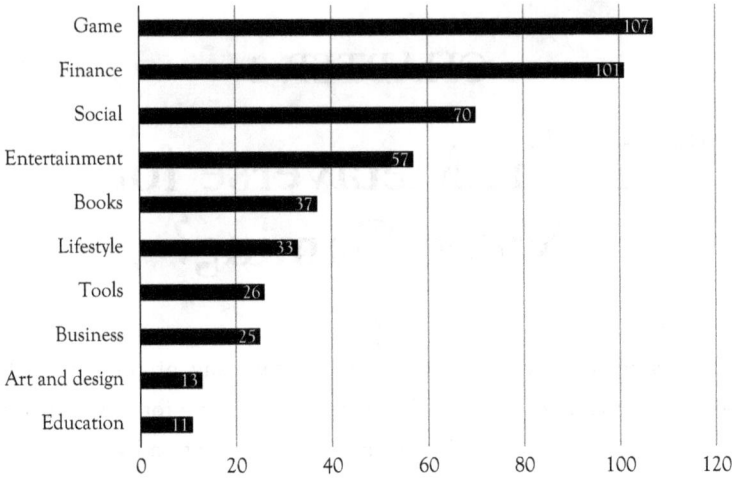

**Figure 2.1** *Top 10 categories per number of apps referencing the Metaverse*

*Source:* Sensor Tower 2022. https://sensortower.com/blog/metaverse-apps/

| Online Game Makers | Design Software Vendors | Social Networking | Gaming, AR, and VR Hardware | Live Entertainment |
|---|---|---|---|---|
| Roblox | Unity | Facebook | Facebook | Live Nation |
| Epic Games | Epic Games | Tencent | Lenovo | Theme Parks |
| Microsoft | Adobe | | HP | Sports Teams |
| Activision Blizzard | Autodesk | | Logitech | |
| Take-Two | Ansys | | Acer | |
| Tencent | | | Valve | |
| NetEase | | | Razer | |
| Nexon | | | | |
| Valve | | | | |

**Figure 2.2** *Metaverse competitive landscape*

*Source:* Influencer Marketing Hub.

the Metaverse is found in Figure 2.2, giving a picture of how the gaming industry dominates this arena.

But, probably, the first one to become famous was Second Life. It provided an environment in which some pioneer explorers of inter-active learning engaged. It proliferated after its launch in 2003 and was used by many users (reaching about a million at the height of its take-up). However, besides being a game, many universities and schools tried their first steps in VR there, and many papers have been published in renowned journals, exploring how Second Life could be used for designing immersive learning environments (De Back et al. 2021), problem-based learning (Sancar-Tokmak and Dogusoy 2020; Dogusoy 2020), or language learning (Parmaxi 2020), for example. Second Life also started stimulating an academic debate among authors about the ethical risks of learning and teaching in inauthentic and game-like environments (Childs et al. 2012). As shown, the first initiatives around the Metaverse were commercially exploited in the video gaming industry but, very soon, further applications were discussed and analyzed by the scientific community.

Recently, two online games are more widely used than Second Life: **Minecraft** and **Roblox**. Both add up to between 150 and 300 million users, most of whom are young and loyal, unlike most who tried Second Life. Both Minecraft and Roblox are **sandbox games**, which means they offer users a VR in which they can build and shape the environment in which they play. This is very different from the ready-made spaces of the shooting and exploring games they supersede. Minecraft is designed for younger players and provides simple blocks to build a shared world. Roblox offers a more programmable environment, providing the makings of a multitude of players' worlds within the game. There has not yet been much academic research around the role of Minecraft and Roblox in other applications besides gaming. Still, it is expected, as they offer an opportunity to explore further applications that could be considered as the seed of the Metaverse.

## What Else Is the Metaverse Expected to Be

But the Metaverse is not just about gaming. In fact, gaming should be considered just a toy model to develop some Metaverse principles and early proof of concepts. As shown in Chapter 1, we are now starting to exploit the first iteration of the Metaverse and doing experiments with the second iteration. The true Metaverse will bring new devices such as contact lenses, wearables, brain–machine connectivity, and much more. And all this will enable an infinite number of new applications. A formal list of the elements of the Metaverse according to Gartner is shown in Figure 2.3.

With all these elements, in a conversation I recently had with Mystakidis (the author of the Metaverse entry in the Encyclopedia seen in Chapter 1), we both agree that the opportunities brought by VR, AR, and extended reality (XR) technologies in general (explained in detail in Chapter 6) will make the Metaverse significantly amplify the capabilities of all "tele" and "e" fields that operate from a distance, like telework, telemedicine, e-business, e-government, e-sports, and e-commerce.

To envision the coming transformation, let's think about the present to envision the future: You will meet your friends or a client in a restaurant. Have you ever used Google Maps or Apple Maps on your smartphone when you are supposed to be around and cannot see it? Or maybe you just used your GPS app, and it brought you exactly to the door? This common use of the technology is possible only because we have small portable devices with a high-resolution display, geolocation satellite systems surrounding planet Earth, broadband wireless networks covering almost any civilized place, and a service provider that adds the points to interest (POIs) on a digital map, and some more technological

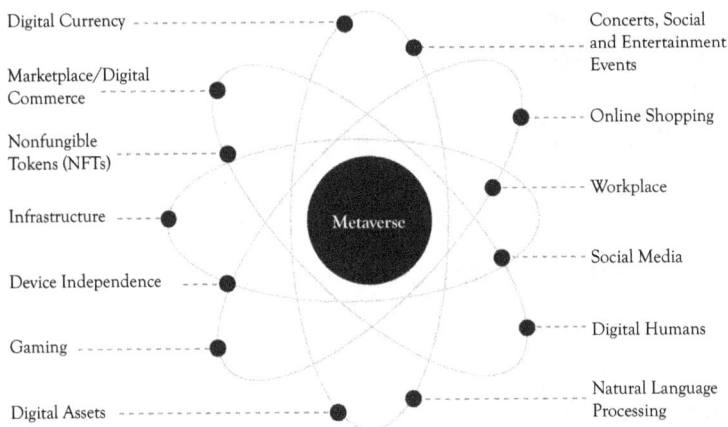

**Figure 2.3 Elements of the Metaverse**

Source: Gartner 2022. https://blogs.gartner.com/robert-hetu/metaverse-implications-for-retail-technology-and-service-providers/

developments. Everything had to exist so you could get to your appointment without trouble.

The same is expected about the Metaverse, once it is mature enough: once the enabling technologies (VR, AR, wearable devices and clothes, brain–machine connectivity, AI, immersive applications by service providers, etc.) are there, the world will be different. Perhaps, in such a disruptive scenario, people will likely prefer to spend more time in the vast *artificial* reality rather than in the "boring" *natural* one. The Metaverse will surely bring the shopping experience to the next level, allowing virtual try of clothing, precise examination of items in the supermarket, including smelling the food or checking the weight and texture of a piece of fruit. It will also change human interaction, making people care more about their digital appeal than their physical one. The Metaverse will transform work, not only by reducing travel by using *telepresence*, as anyone may think, but also by welcoming an alarming number of virtual workers, digital bots, or avatars that work only in the virtual space—the one preferred by most people in the future. So, perhaps when you enter a store in the Metaverse, and you ask the shop assistant about different colors or sizes of an item, that "person" will be a machine, but you will never know that. Or maybe, when you go to a virtual bar to watch a football match with your friends, some of the other people there will be "virtual clients" purchased by the owner to make the bar look more crowded and attract more clients. But, amazingly, you will be able to speak with them, discuss, or mock them as if they were humans' avatars … And you will not notice that they are just AI coded as software. This way, your children's teacher could be a virtual worker in the Metaverse, and even the employee of a company you are trying to contact could be virtual. At some point, the use of deepfake, AR, deep learning, and all edge technologies we have in the experimental phase today will produce a blur between the physical reality and the Metaverse, and it will be tough to distinguish whether you are interacting with a real—physical—object or a digital creation.

The Metaverse will be the door to a world where everything is possible. Beware of that.

## Summary

This chapter has enriched our knowledge about the Metaverse with the following ideas:

- The Metaverse pivots around immersive experiences. The video games industry is one of the most based on experience. Therefore, the Metaverse is rapidly growing in this niche.
- Immersive video games will be used as a toy model to develop further applications in other fields such as remote working, telemedicine, e-sports, e-commerce, e-business, and e-government.
- Video games also provide economy of scale for developing new devices, wearables, VR headsets, and so on, which will contribute to a smooth, progressive evolution to spend more time in the vast *artificial* reality rather than in the "boring" *natural* one.

# CHAPTER 3

# Why the Metaverse Can Change Society for Good

The Metaverse is spatiotemporal. This means that it can be described as a tridimensional space—a virtual space—that evolves on time. It evolves in parallel with the real world but is connected to it. Sensors, machines, and people will be the players of a continuous data flow between the physical reality and the digital one. It opens new habitat for humanity and will bring a different experience to users. At present, Metaverse is in an early development stage, with the Internet, 5G, VR, and other technologies as enablers. The Metaverse has allowed humanity to create a holographic digital world in parallel with the traditional one. And this has never been experienced by any human before.

The Metaverse will not only change the way we do things but also the world as we know it. If past revolutions like the steam machine, electricity, the automobile, and the Internet changed the way people organized their lives and interacted with each other, the Metaverse will be the next revolution. With the implementation of virtual 3D worlds and the services in and around them, we will have infinite possibilities for work, travel, entertainment, research, and more. In this chapter, we will look at some ways we will use the Metaverse once it is ready. Figure 3.1 shows the sectors with a higher expected impact, which will be discussed as follows.

## Entertainment

The entertainment industry is about to undergo one of the most remarkable changes with the upcoming Metaverse. We can expect the entertainment industry to become much more interactive and accessible.

For example, the Metaverse can change the way we listen to music. Artists can create music videos in the Metaverse and sell tickets to their

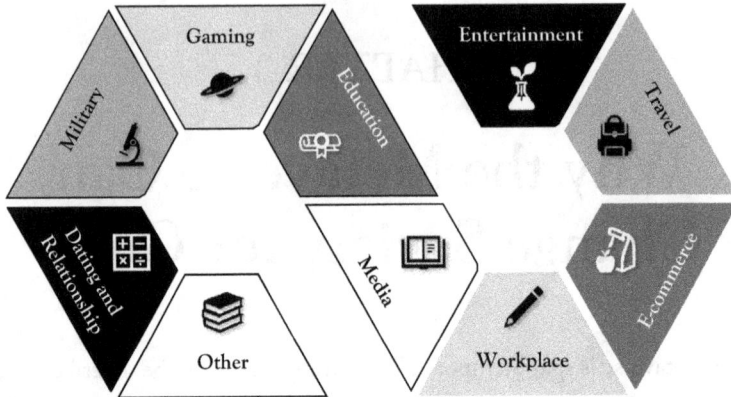

*Figure 3.1 The sectors most impacted by the Metaverse*

studio sessions. We will see artists making 3D music videos, where the audience can experience the music like in a videogame. In addition, the size of the venue will not matter for ticket sales. The Metaverse can take live concerts to the next level: virtual venues can sell the same virtual seat more than once or expand the stands if needed. In addition, people will be able to attend any concert without having to travel, even in time. Anyone could attend a recreation of some famous past shows, like Leonard Cohen's last concert in New Zealand in December 2013, Bob Dylan's performance in Boston Music Hall in November 1975, B.B. King's one in Chicago in September 1970, Elvis' concert in Los Angeles in June 1968, or Jimi Hendrix setting his guitar on fire and smashing it on stage in Monterey, California, June 1967. But this is not all; some recreations could be produced in the Metaverse to attend a concert that never existed, like Frank Sinatra singing in the Colosseum in Rome or Carlos Gardel performing his tangos during the Rockefeller Center Christmas Tree Lighting in New York.

Dramatically, new experiences will come true also in the movie industry. Our favorite movies and television series could easily be immersive, in the sense that you could ride a dragon beside Daenerys Targaryen in Game of Thrones, stay close to Harry Potter while peeking in Hogwarts, or sit in the passenger seat of an Aston Martin, besides 007 driving at full gas—when he has no company. We might see a scenario like this in the more mature stages of the Metaverse. Still, interactive movie experiences are likely to start in the initial stages, given the enormous investments made in this industry. Companies like Disney and Lucas Arts already own the intellectual property rights to their universes, so they are in an excellent position to create their own isolated metaverses, probably in alliance with some top video game developers.

Adult entertainment is another example that is expected to benefit from the Metaverse. Even without knowing exactly how the Metaverse will transform social interaction and relationships, including personal relationships, some reports show that the adult industry is expected to reach $122 billion in 2026. This is nothing new if we analyze the adoption of Internet services in adult entertainment. Another industry that is enthusiastic about the metaverse is the gambling industry. In 2021, online gambling generated $230 billion and remained one of the most lucrative markets for online enterprises. Considering the strategies traditionally followed by casinos to abstract people from reality and immerse them into play, the Metaverse seems even a dangerous place to gamble.

Finally, there will be utterly new entertainment services in the Metaverse. If you go to YouTube and search for "ambience," you will get infinite scenes that show a long sequence (sometimes hours of play) of any place you can dream of (a beach, a castle, a library, an apartment in a skyscraper, etc.). Many people use these ambiences to concentrate or relax. Now imagine this emerging trend developed in a 3D, truly immersive Metaverse. Many people may rearrange their homes to have blank doors on an empty room just to project immersive landscapes or scenes to work, relax, dine, or be with friends.

## Travel

The Metaverse will play an important role in travel in the future. Putting on our glasses will allow us to see anywhere on earth without having to travel. The world of 3D modeling and rendering has changed drastically over the past decade. In the past, rendering and shading realistic 3D models was highly resource-intensive, resulting in heavy graphics. Nowadays, we have better 3D production methods, and our graphic cards and Internet connection also process them much more quickly and efficiently. Leading companies like Unity and NVIDIA are already developing cutting-edge 3D visual technologies that look incredibly real-istic. These graphics are currently used mainly in video games. Still, they are gradually being introduced to the movie industry, and some initiatives are also available in the cultural sector, making it possible to visit famous museums or historical places. Very soon, we will have video services that let us travel anywhere in the world without leaving home. Better yet, we won't have to deal with crowded landmarks and may choose the weather we love for each moment.

But there will be more than just travel in the Metaverse. One of the most exciting features the Metaverse will offer is time travel. By recreating any past location, either using recorded images, photos, or recreations using 3D images of objects and places, some places like Pompei could be visited right hours before Vesuvius started eruption. Or we could sail on the Santa Maria with Christopher Columbus in his travel from Spain to the discovery of the New World.

Additionally, Metaverse travel will be perfect for those who love travel but are limited somehow. Professionals who work full-time and have lim-ited time off, parents who cannot travel with young children, older people who have physical limitations, people with disabilities, and people who are not allowed visas to visit some countries are examples of lives the Metaverse travel will change.

## E-Commerce

Web 2.0 (the interactive web) has made e-commerce popular. Numer-ous retail business owners transitioned to digital, and many new entrants developed lucrative e-commerce stores. The push given by the Covid-19 pandemic has made online deliveries become the norm and develop the whole e-commerce ecosystem at a very fast pace. But we can expect our online shopping habits to evolve much more with the arrival of the Metaverse. Stores will be able to open a 3D shop in a virtual shopping mall. Using our 3D glasses or kits, we will be able to walk into these stores and check out the actual size, color, and fit before we make the purchase.

On the other side, shopping will take place in the VR economy itself: virtual land, objects, nonfungible tokens (NFTs), and other goods will be available to us. Even payments could be made using cryptocurrencies like bitcoin, Ethereum, or any other. Many questions arise in e-commerce when entering the Metaverse, like how would virtual shops be? For example, consider that users navigate the Metaverse usually through an avatar, and size is not standard in a sense we as humans understand. An avatar can be 6, 3, or 10 feet tall. Most retailers put products at a certain height on shelves depending on those with higher margin (aligned with the visual line), those in a sale (nearly below), cheaper ones (on the lower shelves, so you must crouch to take them), and luxury ones (a bit above the visual line, so they seem more inaccessible). What will happen when an avatar can have such a discrepancy in size?

Additionally, the effort to make items available for purchase is higher than in Web 2.0 because 3D rendering is needed and, probably, weight, texture, and so on will be added in the future. Soft objects, like clothes, will need even further evolution to let users experience bending, texture, and fitting in a virtual space.

## Workplace

Several tech giants like Microsoft have been working on creating a metaverse for the workplace. The initial plan is to create virtual conference rooms where colleagues could meet using VR. During the pandemic, online meetings have become commonplace in the workplace using apps like Zoom, Teams, and Google Meet. Employees have felt the effects of what is called "Zoom fatigue," and companies are looking for better ways to engage employees online.

Through the Metaverse, an online conference room will become much more realistic. The presentations will be more compelling, communication will feel more natural, and the audience will feel closer, physically. One of the major consequences is that, as Metaverse workplaces prove to be helpful, the number of international and remote teams will increase. Furthermore, companies can hold their meetings online and reduce their travel expenses. Even though the Metaverse will not wholly emulate the human interaction in a physical environment, at least in the initial stages, it will provide additional benefits like simultaneous translation for international meetings or minimizing commuting time.

## Media

One of the major side effects of Web 2.0 is that, supported by the ability of the end-user to interact with service providers, now the Internet allows users not only to consume but also to generate information. Among the most significant reflections of this fact are social media. This possibility makes the Internet give alternative media a fair chance to compete with mass media. As a result, the press and TV networks struggle to keep the oligopoly they have enjoyed for decades.

It is hard to predict what Web 3.0 will bring to the table as far as the media is concerned. Media outlets on the entertainment side might find it easier to adapt to the Metaverse. However, it remains unclear how the news channels will evolve. Governments will no doubt act against the complete decentralization of news, as they do today. However, self-journalism and social media may become more prominent as people become more immersed in VR and get used to a-la-carte services. We will likely have more access to personal news stories that AI thinks we will be interested in. To date, *Time* magazine has taken the boldest step into the Metaverse from a media outlet. They are launching a weekly newsletter solely dedicated to the Metaverse.

## Education

The Covid-19 pandemic has proven that face-to-face education is not the only way to learn. While online education has its challenges and setbacks, the Metaverse will offer some solutions. Using the Metaverse, teachers can interact with children in VR, sharing space, gestures, and context far better than using videoconference. Even more impressive, a teacher will be able to instruct any student who does not share the same language by employing machine learning (ML) techniques and real-time translation technologies.

The Metaverse has the potential to revolutionize education. Instead of using textbooks with images or multimedia content in the current online education, teachers could instantly immerse students in the scenes of study (imagine the implications for learning architecture, medicine, history, biology, and all disciplines).

We can expect schools worldwide to evolve their virtual campuses to *metaverse campuses* in the future. A few examples are already underway. For instance, a virtual campus will be created at the Kenya-KAIST campus, which is expected to open by September 2023 in the Konza Technopolis. The University of Nicosia is preparing to open the first permanent university gallery for NFTs. Over time, these examples will multiply and become more complex, resulting in student exchange programs being a daily occurrence. If online education is already questioning why people must study in a specific place, the Metaverse will likely change that trend for good, as geographical location will probably become almost irrelevant to study in any place on any subject. And this may likely change the university map worldwide, probably leading to a consolidation of large universities and the progressive disappearance of the smaller ones. Like in other large revolutions, technology will transform the roots of society to a certain level.

Another group that will benefit from the educational implementation of the Metaverse is students with disabilities. It will be easier for teachers to design personalized activities for disabled students, and long-term hospitalization will not hinder academic success as much.

## Gaming

Gaming will be one of the industries to first cross the frontier into the Metaverse. VR glasses caught the gaming industry's attention when they were introduced. Some popular game engines like Unity 3D offer developers to adapt their games to VR already. Moreover, 3D art and environments have been used in the industry for decades, which makes things easier to transition to the new Metaverse era. Games with large followings, such as MMORPGs and MOBAs, have utilized their own currencies for in-game purchases for a long time. A few developers are now accepting cryptocurrency payments too.

The gaming industry has all these advantages over other industries, making it one of the early birds for Web 3.0. From the most prominent game studios shifting toward the Metaverse to small start-ups making developments in 3D modeling or VR, the gaming industry will surely be one of the drivers to shape the Metaverse in the next years.

## Military

The military has always been an early investor in technology, although most of its inventions typically remain secret for some time to keep an advantage over potential enemies. Keeping up with the latest technology is necessary for the armed forces to stay in top shape. In addition, armed forces around the world rely more and more on simulations to train their personnel. Because the Metaverse will create realistic simulations, it is natural for the military industry to take advantage of it. Optimus System was one of the first companies to jump on board. This company develops and supplies military training simulators. DEIMOS, its new Metaverse technology, is preparing to enter the global market. The system creates military training environments for precision shooting, tactical behavior training, and observation training.

Military war games and training cost organizations like NATO billions of dollars annually. With the help of Metaverse technologies, not only would these organizations be able to reduce their budget, but they could also increase the quality of the training and add more variables to study human behavior under the pressure of war through biometric data collection and integration in the simulation.

## Dating and Relationships

Online dating has changed the way people meet. Nowadays, meeting someone is as simple as logging onto a website or downloading an app on your phone. We can only anticipate the Metaverse to shake things up even more. Remember that AI, especially in the form of ML, is a crucial part of dating applications like Tinder or OkCupid to match each user with other people that share some interests. This not only saves time but also increases the chances of a first date going well.

We can expect to see the same applications on a larger scale once the Metaverse starts spreading among the population. However, dating will start happening in the virtual space, which implies certain differences, like not having to share some personal information like the phone number. This should make online dating a safer experience in the future.

Additionally, it will make a date possible for long-distance couples. Some couples start off long-distance, and some evolve into long-distance relationships due to work, like army officers, pilots, or international business executives. The Metaverse era will give these people a chance to be virtually together for dinner or watching a movie, even when they are thousands of miles away.

## Other Transformations

There is no doubt that the Metaverse will impact all industries one way or another. We have mentioned the ones more likely to experience profound changes with the expansion of the Metaverse. However, other sectors will experience significant changes as well. Art, for example, will benefit from the 3D representation of objects to show and analyze antiquities, tribal objects, and so on without the risk of deterioration, or navigate through archaeological places such as the Tomb of Tutankhamun or Pompei without the need to travel or the access restrictions those places may have. Additionally, many museums that must keep many artworks stored in the basement because of lack of space could virtually show them in the Metaverse and make additional profit or increase their reputation.

In the health care sector, using virtual spaces to let the surgeon analyze the patient and simulate the surgical operation before entering the operating room will multiply the availability of this scarce and expensive resource while reducing the dose of anesthesia, minimizing the risk for the patient.

In the same way, in the industry, as an evolution of Industry 4.0—where industrial machines are connected to the Internet to process and analyze the sensor data and improve the processes—the Metaverse will offer many possibilities with the use of AR and VR to test, simulate, and build better algorithms without interfering the production line, and facilitating remote operation in hazardous environments.

These are just some examples to illustrate how the Metaverse will enter all of our lives. In this scenario, it is essential to respond on time. By embracing the Metaverse early on and exploring its potential, we can take advantage of this wonderful technology and not let it pass us by as it changes the world.

# Summary

In this chapter, we have seen how the Metaverse will transform everything. The main ideas are summarized as follows:

- The Metaverse will open a new habitat for humanity with much more possibilities than we enjoy in the physical world.
- All industries will be able to develop new services and experiences in the Metaverse, leading to a complete social transformation.
- The entertainment industry will not be limited by a flat screen and the interaction with keyboards, buttons, and *scrolls*.
- The travel sector will offer not only physical travels but also virtual ones, travels enriched with augmented reality, and "time travels."
- E-commerce will not just consist of scrolling through a table of pictures of different items but manipulating them in our hands, *feeling* them, and entering virtual stores as we do with physical ones.
- The media industry will be entirely transformed by monetized user-generated content and artificial-intelligence-generated content. It is difficult to tell what will happen with news, information, and disinformation.
- The gaming industry will be the most important for fulfilling people's leisure time, providing a way of evasion to a much more attractive *reality*.
- The military sector will benefit from virtual worlds to be more effective and reduce costs. The war will also be fought in the Metaverse in the future.
- Dating and relationships will dramatically change, making distant relatives closer and allowing much more *granularity* when sharing personal or private information (even our hair color) with others.
- All other industries will also transform because of the Metaverse: health care, manufacturing, education, and so on.

# CHAPTER 4

# Who Is Behind It

Some countries started earlier than others to regulate and publish policies for the use or promotion of the Metaverse, mainly the United States, China, Japan, South Korea, and the United Arab Emirates (UAE). Most of them, like the Office of the National Coordinator for Health Information Technology in the United States and the UAE Securities and Commodities Authority (SCA), have mainly addressed questions related to Blockchain technology. Still, some countries like South Korea want to play an active role in the Metaverse industry. For such, the Korean Office of Technology and Standards started to consider the field of the Metaverse early in 2021.

Besides that, it is expected that the largest standards associations (e.g., ITU, IEEE, IET, and WWW) play an active role in the continuous regulation of the Metaverse as independent international entities that help the entire technology ecosystem interact and build solutions that can leverage on others.

But, as usual, money goes where business is and vice versa, and the technology roadmap of the Metaverse, shown in Figure 4.1, can probably give more specific clues about who is really making an effort to bring the true Metaverse to reality. We must realize that, although most companies embrace the Metaverse's concepts and vision, cautions and doubts also emerge. For instance, while **Apple** and **Microsoft** have virtual space applications, they consider that seamlessly connecting the Metaverse and the physical world with proper devices is a key to their success. This is still a challenge, given the limitations in hardware that we have already mentioned. And they see that solving this challenge could be more important than developing the Metaverse itself. They believe that the purpose of creating virtual spaces is mainly intended to enable people to improve productivity, communicate, and reduce production costs in the physical world.

According to this scheme, it is easy to guess who is or is expected to be behind it, understood as the forces investing and doing research to bring solutions and new technology that bring us to the next iteration of the

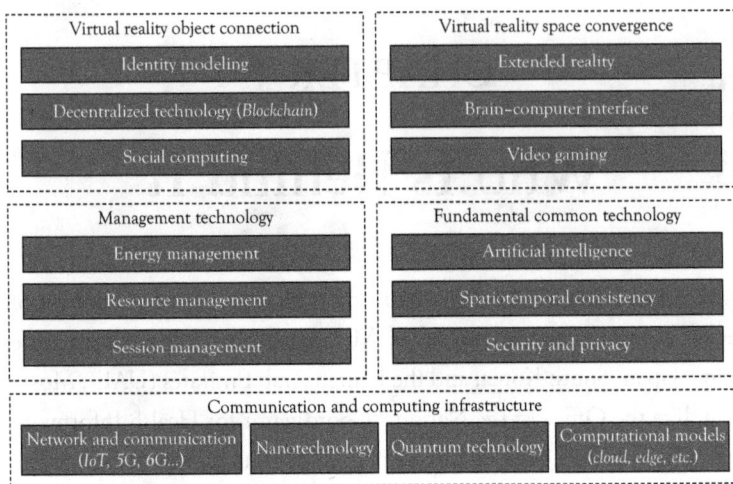

| Virtual reality object connection | Virtual reality space convergence |
|---|---|
| Identity modeling | Extended reality |
| Decentralized technology (*Blockchain*) | Brain–computer interface |
| Social computing | Video gaming |

| Management technology | Fundamental common technology |
|---|---|
| Energy management | Artificial intelligence |
| Resource management | Spatiotemporal consistency |
| Session management | Security and privacy |

| Communication and computing infrastructure | | | |
|---|---|---|---|
| Network and communication (*IoT, 5G, 6G...*) | Nanotechnology | Quantum technology | Computational models (*cloud, edge, etc.*) |

*Figure 4.1 Technology roadmap of the Metaverse adapted from H. Ning et al. (2021)*

Metaverse. Speaking with Paul (Lik-Hang) Lee from the Korea Advanced Institute of Science and Technology (KAIST), one of the leading institutions investing in the development of the Metaverse, he highlights the fact that "there is still no definitive answer to the ultimate form of the Metaverse, although it can be regarded as immersive cyberspace." Mr. Lee believes that Meta, Snapchat, and Niantic are significant players focusing on diversified types of immersive cyberspace. Meta owns the capability of hardware (e.g., Oculus headsets) and software development (e.g., Horizon) to develop the next generation of immersive social platforms in 3D virtual worlds. Snap Inc. offers an XR development framework, namely Lens Studio, to invite multitudinous content creators to enrich physical worlds. Finally, Niantic uses smartphones to bring digital entities superimposing on top of physical environments. Its most remarkable app is the game Pokemon Go, with more than 1 billion downloads.

In the following sections, a more thorough analysis of the largest investors in each region of the world is performed.

## The United States

Going specific to who is behind the investments to make the Metaverse a reality, there are some representative companies already investing and positioned in the first stage of the development of the Metaverse. Most of them are U.S. multinational companies, as one may imagine, given the current technological landscape:

- **Meta**: Formerly called Facebook, in September 2019, Meta released the VR social platform "Facebook Horizon" and launched a public beta in August 2020. In July 2021, the company announced that it would transform into a Metaverse company within five years, investing at least $10 billion in its "Reality Labs" project. In Autumn 2021, the company changed its name to "Meta" and released its beta version of the "Meta" metaverse, with very limited functionality. In 2022, the company also changed the brand of its recently acquired company from "Oculus" to "Meta" as well. Although there are still very limited developments on the Meta metaverse, an important evolution is expected in the next months and years, given that the company also has VR headsets to provide an end-to-end experience to users.
- **Nvidia**: The company announced a plan to create the first virtual collaboration and simulation platform called "Omniverse" in August 2021. This platform can be used to connect 3D worlds into a shared virtual space and create digital twins, simulating real-world buildings and factories. Omniverse has three key components: the first one is Omniverse Nucleus, a database engine that allows multiple users to connect and create a scene together; the second one is the rendering and animation engine to simulate the virtual world, and the third one is Nvidia CloudXR for streaming XR content to client devices. Meanwhile, Omniverse integrates AI to train digital twins in the Metaverse.
- **Roblox**: It is another gaming company heavily investing in developing Metaverse games. As the largest user-generated content (UGC) game platform, players in Roblox can create their own games and virtual worlds. They can buy, sell, and create virtual items that can be used to decorate

their avatars. Roblox supports VR devices to enhance user immersion but provides limited XR support, as it is just designed as a game. However, Roblox is currently one of the virtual worlds that have the potential to be closest to the Metaverse concept.

- **Epic Games**: This gaming company is famous for its game engine Unreal. In its most popular game, Fortnite, regarded as a prototype of the Metaverse, users can create their avatars, buy digital items, and enjoy movies and concerts. In April 2021, Epic Games announced a $1 billion investment to build a metaverse and acquired Skethfab, the largest platform for 3D models, to absorb user traffic from this platform and increase its market share in the Metaverse business.

- **Amazon**: Since 2018, Amazon has been developing a "new VR shopping experience" and trying to target the Metaverse to create a virtual shopping space where shoppers can interact with digital products. This company is building a kind of virtual 3D "Amazon shopping mall" in the Metaverse to assert its dominant position in the retail sector by extrapolating it to the virtual space. Although most of these developments have not been fully disclosed by the company yet, some features are already available. Its newest AR shopping tool, "Room Decorator," allows you to use your phone or tablet to see what furniture and other home decoration will look like in your space. You can view multiple products together and even save the AR snapshots of your room for later review.

- **Disney**: The company has already experimented with some Metaverse founding technologies, like NFTs, in the series of "Golden Moments" NFTs resembling statues inspired by stories from Disney, Pixar, Star Wars, and Marvel. But Disney is a major player in this arena, not just for this. Nvidia Omniverse platform, mentioned earlier, uses a standard open language called "Universal Scene Description" (USD), provided by Disney's branch Pixar.

Besides its technological leadership, Disney is probably the closest business to feelings, emotions, visual content, and entertainment. And this is expected to be one of its major assets in entering the Metaverse. Disney executives are thinking about ways to connect better physical spaces like Disneyland parks with digital ventures such as the Disney+ streaming service, as well as virtual environments as they emerge. How, for example, could Disney+ and Genie, Disneyland's app for guidance and on-site navigation, work together to make a complete experience? Disney's CEO, Bob Chapek, speaks of the new development saying that "it's going to take all the great things that we as a media company have with Disney+ and use that as a platform for the Metaverse. But at the same time, we have something that no one else has, and that's the physical world, the world of our parks. And so, if the Metaverse is blending the physical and the digital in one environment, who can do it better than Disney?"

- **Snap Inc**: With some solutions like Lens Studio (or Snap AR), already mentioned, and Snapchat, this is one important vendor to watch. Snapchat introduced custom avatars and filters to fill the world with digital content. It also launched the Bitmoji service, which allows users to pose in physical snapshots and create their own 3D Bitmoji avatars. Although it is probably not a significant contribution to bringing the Metaverse closer, it is worth mentioning it as a large investment venture.

- **Decentraland**: A VR virtual world based on Ethereum, it was the first fully decentralized virtual world owned by users. The core content of Decentraland is artwork, and there is a place dedicated to the exhibition of digital artwork. Although investments are expected to be much lower than the ones already mentioned, some large firms are developing their virtual worlds in Decentraland, like Samsung, shown in the following.

## South Korea

Another important country where large public and private investments are being made in relation to the Metaverse is South Korea. There are four relevant organizations related to the Metaverse industry:

- **Samsung**: Samsung is progressively evolving its products and strategy toward the Metaverse. Its smart TVs started to be equipped with NFT support to show graphical NFT material. The company also opened a virtual store in Decentraland, called "Samsung 837X," like a digital version of its physical store "Samsung 837." Around this, the company released its own social network related to its virtual store, called "Discord." But besides being a technological giant, Samsung is a global financial player through Samsung Asset Management, South Korea's biggest asset manager, which launched the "Samsung Global Metaverse Fund." This fund invests in eight themes: cloud computing, VR, online gaming, online payments, 3D design tools, platform businesses, mobility, and the luxury goods industry.
- **SK Telecom**: In July 2021, SK Telecom introduced a virtual world called "ifland," where users can host and participate in meetings through cartoon characters. *ifland* offers a range of features for social networking and is growing into a globally accessible service fueled by cooperation with various partners. SK Telecom has developed proprietary technologies in AR and VR and expects to use *ifland* as the test bed for them.
- **Urbanbase**: It is a 3D spatial data platform for real estate and interior design development. The company raised 13 billion won (more than 10 million U.S. dollars) in the B+ funding round to develop VR, AR, and 3D technologies for Business-to-Business (B2B) applications. It is expected to be one of the technology developers of Metaverse applications over the next coming years.
- **Metaverse Alliance**: The Korean Information and Communications Industry Promotion Agency gathered

25 large organizations and companies in the country to form the Metaverse Alliance. The goal of this initiative is to build the Metaverse ecosystem under the leadership of the private sector through government and business collaboration, to propose and develop an open Metaverse platform, and let South Korea and its companies become world leaders and the reference for Metaverse future expansion and adoption.

# China

As another technology giant country, China also has large companies making huge investments to grow faster toward the Metaverse:

- **Tencent**: It is one of the highest-grossing multimedia companies in the world based on revenue. It is also the largest company in the video game industry in the world based on its investments. Tencent has made a whole series of investments in the Metaverse ecosystem, including an AR development platform, a game called "Avakin life," a music streaming platform, and so on. However, not much is disclosed about its roadmap for evolving its portfolio and customers to the Metaverse.
- **Alibaba**: Although not much has been disclosed about Alibaba's strategy regarding the Metaverse, the company applied for the registration of some trademarks such as "Ali Metaverse" and "Taobao Metaverse." In 2022, to prepare for the country's annual 618 Shopping Festival, Alibaba's Taobao company released a virtual shopping venue open to its customers. Using their phones, shoppers could guide their avatars through 3D stores and engage in several interactive activities. According to the company, the project is used to undergo a technical exploration of the immersive shopping scenarios the Metaverse offers.
- **HTC** (Taiwan): HTC became famous long ago for its handhelds or Personal Digital Assistants (PDAs). The mobile device manufacturer is now returning with strength,

producing new devices for the Metaverse, which include blockchain support and smooth connectivity to HTC's own metaverse, called "VIVERSE." According to the company, "VIVERSE provides an array of tools, services, and platforms for individuals, enterprises, creators, and developers to enrich this new immersive space."

- **NetEase**: NetEase's layout of the Metaverse focuses on the game business and provides low-threshold tools for game development. This company invested in a Metaverse computing platform called "Improbable" to enable third parties to build virtual worlds and a social network specialized in creating virtual characters called "IMVU."

- **ByteDance**: This company owns high-traffic platforms such as Douyin. It has invested in visual computing and the AI computing platform called "Moore Thread." ByteDance released the game "Restart the World" and acquired PICO, a Chinese VR equipment company.

- **ZQGame**: This brand is a trendsetting Chinese game studio. In September 2021, ZQGame released the game "Brew Master" preview. This game allows players to start businesses in a simulated environment and experience the real-life impact. As an example, ZQGame plans to use its game to take players back to China a hundred years ago and let them run a winery. What is unique from other games is that the company plans to cooperate with an actual winery, so players can get the wines they make in the game world delivered to their real homes.

- **Wondershare Technology**: This giant, the developer of the Filmora video suite, has invested in Realibox to enhance its business layout in the AR and VR field and provide a solid technical foundation for the initial deployment of the Metaverse. As a global leader in creative software development, Wondershare also built the "Wondershare Creator Club" in The Sandbox metaverse, providing creators with more opportunities to monetize their passion as the Metaverse becomes more popular.

# Europe

Europe is not known for being an early adopter, *traditionally*. Therefore, limited initiatives are being seriously accomplished by European companies. Some examples are as follows:

- **Maze Theory** (the UK): The famous British VR studio Maze Theory will create a "fan metaverse" around well-known characters, themes, and other fan universes (e.g., the "Dr. Who" series).
- **Stage11** (France): This music platform closed a €5 million funding round led by the European venture capital fund "Otium Capital" to create immersive Metaverse music.
- **Gucci** (Italy): The famous luxury brand Gucci has launched virtual sports shoes. After purchasing the shoes, consumers can use them in the Gucci App and on some VR social platforms like VR Chat or try them out on the game platform Roblox.

# Japan

Three Japanese companies have made significant investments related to the Metaverse:

- **Sony**: Sony is the owner of PlayStation, which puts this company in an excellent position to explore the Metaverse through gaming. But the company's most significant strategic movement may be its close partnership with Epic Games, the engine maker of Unreal Game, which is known for enabling the industry's most advanced gaming titles. As a hardware manufacturer, Sony is also developing its own VR headsets to compete directly with Meta.
- **GREE**: This company has been operating the famous social network in Japan, "Gree," since 2004. It started operating "REALITY," a virtual live streaming application built for smartphones. With just a phone, anyone can turn himself

into a digital avatar and stream all kinds of content. Streamers can host live digital performances, play games, and even just chat without showing their faces. It is estimated that 10 billion yen (around 75 million U.S. dollars) will be invested by 2024 to develop more than 100 million users worldwide.

- **Virtual Avex Group**: It is a Japanese entertainment conglomerate that has shifted into other business domains such as anime, video games, and live music events. Avex plans to promote existing animation or game characters, host virtual artist activities, and virtualize concerts by real artists and other activities.

## Summary

In this chapter, we have seen specific companies and players already investing in the Metaverse. Let's summarize the most essential ideas as follows:

- The Metaverse is now taking shape. Although isolated experiments happened in the past, now large corporations and standards associations are investing and working seriously.
- The technological giants Facebook, Apple, Microsoft, Google, Amazon … are heavily investing in developing Metaverse applications or devices.
- Regarding countries, the United States has the longest list of large corporations investing in the Metaverse, with popular names like Nvidia, Epic Games, and Disney, and some less famous but with specific developments for the Metaverse, like Roblox, Snap Inc., and Decentraland.
- South Korea is strongly focusing on becoming a Metaverse leader, and some companies like Samsung, SK Telecom, and Urbanbase are investing large sums in the development of Metaverse applications, services, and devices. Additionally, the South Korean government created the Metaverse Alliance to let 25 large Korean companies work jointly to make the country a world reference.

- China has a vast potential to become a Metaverse leader, with large corporations like Tencent, Alibaba, HTC, NetEase, ByteDance, ZQGame, and Wondershare investing already.
- Europe and Japan are two relevant economies with some exciting initiatives around the Metaverse.

# CHAPTER 5

# How Is the Metaverse Built

The Metaverse is still under discussion and will surely be for several years because it is a new paradigm of accessing digital information using emerging and other technologies that do not even exist today. Consequently, there are different approaches to describing the components of the Metaverse. For instance, Tan Ping, the person in charge of XR Lab at the Chinese company Alibaba, makes a model heavily based on visual inputs by dividing the Metaverse into four layers: L1 (holographic construction), L2 (holographic simulation), L3 (virtual and real fusion), and L4 (virtual and real linkage).

However, owing to the interdisciplinary nature of the Metaverse, we prefer the model described in Figure 5.1, which has 14 areas under two key categories: technologies and ecosystem. These key technologies fuel the "Digital Big Bang" from the Internet and VR to the Metaverse.

Under the technology category, there are eight pillars. Users can access the Metaverse through XR and techniques for user interactivity (e.g., manipulating virtual objects). Computer vision, artificial intelligence (AI), Blockchain, and robotics/Internet of Things (IoT) can work with the user to handle various activities inside the Metaverse through user interactivity and XR. Edge computing (placing as much processing power in users' devices or sensors instead of using the computer's CPU or cloud computing resources) aims to improve the performance of applications sensitive to latency and bandwidth. In contrast, cloud computing is well-recognized for its highly scalable computational power and storage capacity. Leveraging both cloud-based and edge-based services can achieve synergy, such as maximizing application performance and hence user experience. Accordingly, edge devices and cloud services with advanced mobile networks can support computer vision, AI, robotics, and IoT, on top of appropriate hardware infrastructure.

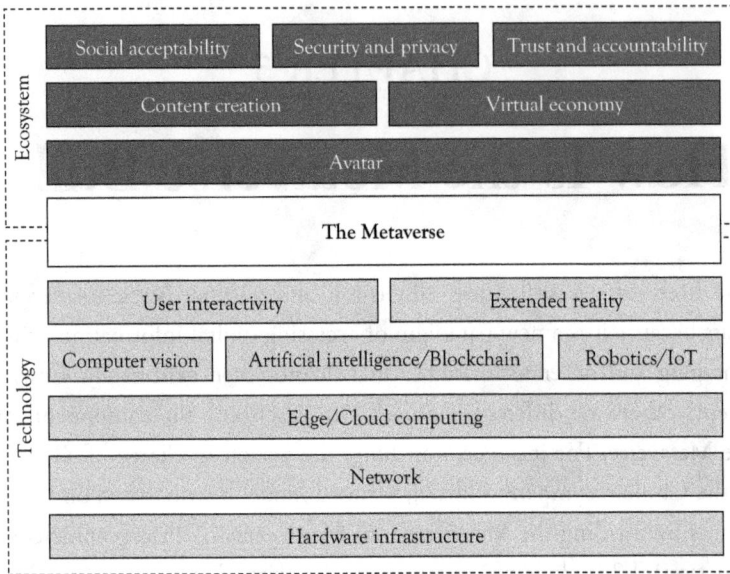

**Figure 5.1 The 14 areas of the Metaverse, under two fundamental categories**

Source: Lee et al. 2021.

The ecosystem category describes an independent virtual world mirroring the real world. Users in the physical world can control their avatars through XR and user interaction techniques for various collective activities such as content creation. Therefore, the virtual economy is a spontaneous derivative of such activities in the Metaverse. We consider three focused areas of social acceptability: security, privacy, and trust and accountability. Analog to society in the physical world, content creation, and virtual economy should align with the social norms and regulations. For instance, the production in the virtual economy should be protected by ownership, while such production outcomes should be accepted by others in the Metaverse. Also, users would expect that their activities are not exposed to privacy risks and security threats, which will be addressed in Chapter 7.

Besides the relatively large number of components—14—considered in this model for the Metaverse, for the purposes of this book, we will follow a classical but still helpful approach to the components of the Metaverse found in (Park and Kim 2022). This model follows a more straightforward approach to better understand how the Metaverse is built, considering the whole Metaverse as a combination of hardware, software, and content.

## Hardware Enabling the Metaverse

Specific hardware for the Metaverse is key to providing an immersive experience, as standard access to the Internet consists mainly of flat displays that cannot offer such an experience. At the same time, hardware is a technically limiting barrier owing to the high demand for computing power (especially for 3D graphic rendering). Hardware for the Metaverse is thus on the technological edge and quickly enhanced by the effects of technological advancement.

The interaction hardware for the Metaverse must meet the following conditions:

- The interactive device is lightweight, convenient, wearable, and portable.
- The transparency of the interactive device allows users to ignore the traces of technology and better immerse themselves in the virtual world.

The essential hardware to access the Metaverse is a head-mounted display (HMD), commonly called "virtual reality glasses." Critical factors for such a physical device are the resolution (how many pixels for a given visual field angle are provided), the field of view size (the wider the field, the more immersive the experience), and latency (the delay between the image is produced in the computer and shown to the user). As you may guess, the higher the resolution is, the more realistic the vision is, which complements the field of view size to simulate that we are *there*. However, increasing each of these parameters also increases the amount of data (bits) transmitted between the application and the HMD device, which leads to an increase in latency, giving the sense of a "slow-motion reality," destroying the utility of immersive experience when user interaction is required. The increase in computing power and higher bandwidth connections periodically brought by newer technologies make the immersive experience better over time.

## HMDs

An HMD shows two synchronized images, one to each user's eye, to give the impression of a 3D vision. As shown in Figure 5.2, our left and right eyes will perceive a different image depending on the distance an object is placed regarding the observer. With these two images, the brain makes the rest, detecting matched items in each image and calculating their distance (you were unaware of the millions of calculations your brain does each time you open your eyes, eh?).

An HMD can also include a headset for stereo audio listening. Audio does not represent any significant technological challenge because it is much less demanding than video.

HMDs are categorized into nonsee-through HMD, optical-see-through HMD, and video-see-through HMD (Ruffner et al 2004). In the case of a method that covers the screen, it provides a sense of immersion in a completely virtual world (VR). Optical-see-through (mainly used in AR) is a method of overlaying information and artificial objects in the real world and requires high hardware specifications to properly do the overlaying, first detecting and interpreting the physical reality recorded by the cameras or other types of sensors and then to place the digital information over it, in the proper moving position.

To complement this method, video-see-through HMD is used. In this modality, a full video representation is produced, partially coming from recording the real scene and adding extra information or virtual

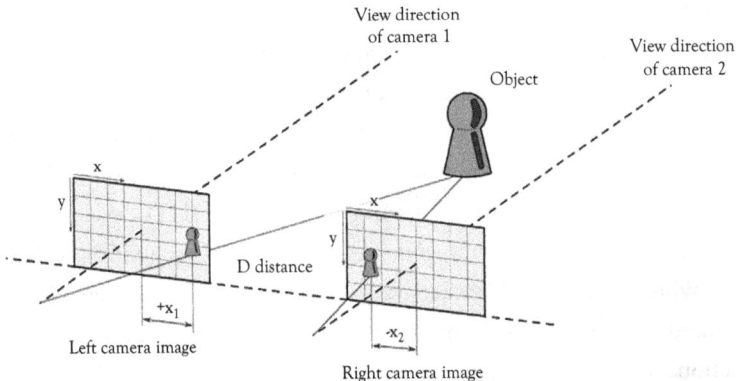

*Figure 5.2 Perception of distance using two cameras (or eyes)*

objects, instead of using a transparent glass that lets the user see reality through it. What application could that technology have? Suppose you are a pilot, and you could see around through a 360-degree camera placed outside the plane, with overlayed information about the destination, the landing track, and so on. Or you could be driving a tank from the inside with no windows while seeing everything.

### Hand Tracking Devices

We usually do most of the interaction with the real world using our hands. We need to do the same in the Metaverse, and, for that, there are some technologies developed. The simplest one is using wireless remote controllers that can be grabbed with each hand, equipped with motion sensors (orientation, accelerometers, impact, and even buttons), like the one used by the famous Meta Quest (formerly Oculus Quest) (Figure 5.3).

This device technology where people interact directly with their body without any complex or indirect movements (like in the case of a joystick) is called "somatosensory technology." More complex somatosensory technologies use a camera to monitor hand movements, like the one being developed by Manomotion (Figure 5.4). Or even grabbing

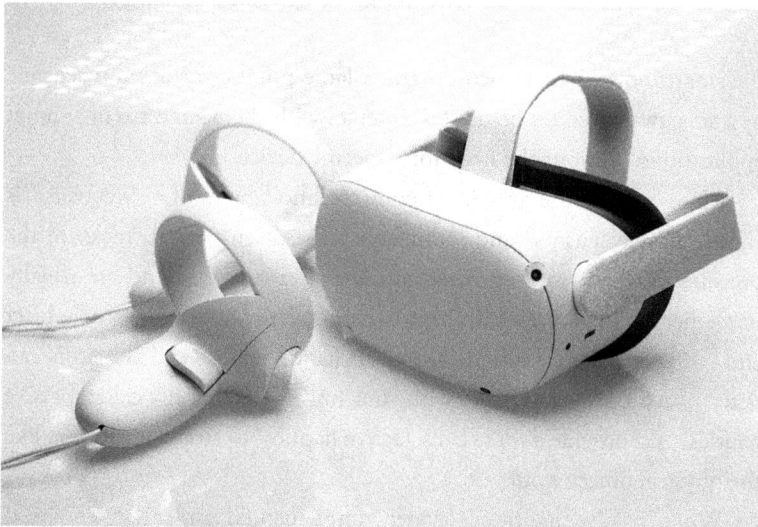

*Figure 5.3  Hand tracking device used by the Meta Quest set*

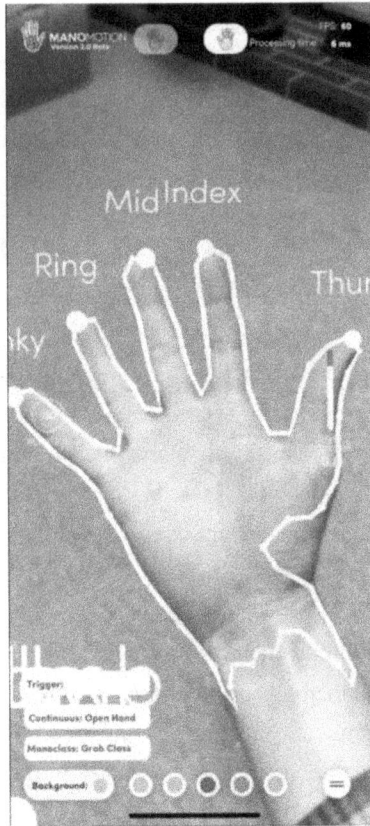

*Figure 5.4 Manomotion moving hand recognition technology*

the smartphone, which incorporates a large number of motion sensors, or a smartwatch could be used to interact with the Metaverse in simpler applications, without the need for a specific device.

More advanced hand interaction technology in the Metaverse is called "haptic sensors" and "actuators." These sensors can measure the pressure on them or even make pressure over a surface and are usually implemented in gloves. With haptic sensors, one can grab a virtual object and feel as if it were really there, in our hand. Sensors and actuators can detect the pressure you make with your fingers (technically called passive haptics) and provide a force back (active haptics) to stop your fingers like the physical object would do.

While passive haptics is widely implemented and relatively inex-pensive (e.g., the Apple Pencil or the MacBook touchpad are equipped with haptic sensors to detect different pressure levels), adding force-back actuators is much more complicated and the existing solutions are still bulky and experimental. However, some advances are being made toward providing texture feeling by applying micro-force patterns to the fingertips, which has limited applications but could be the origin of a new set of services (an example of this is the virtual central button of the iPhone 7 and some later models, where a small mechanical pulse gives the impression of pushing a physical button).

### Other Input Devices

Many technologies can be used to interact in the Metaverse. Some of them, like voice recognition, are widely known, but others, such as eye tracking or head tracking, are not so common. Eye tracking is a method of changing the viewpoint or the mouse arrow by following the eye movement, typically using a camera to record the user's face. It is a technology that allows the user to look in different directions to take some actions on a display or a virtual world. In the Metaverse applications, it has the advantage of reducing the load on image processing by generating high-resolution images only in the section where the user is effectively looking, following a fovea-like method.[1]

A next step toward integrating our physical movement into the Metaverse, providing effective use of the physical sense of space or gravity, is body tracking and treadmill, which can be used to provide accurate motion information with auxiliary devices. Motion input devices are also divided into those that use a passive method and those that use an active method. The passive method delivers a sense to the user with a fixed scenario, so the user movements are normally limited. For example, let's imagine a game where the player is in a 3D world, and the system always orients the player avatar toward the right path. This way, the user will only need to move his arms or head, not his whole body. The active

---

[1] The eye fovea is a central section of the inner eye that presents a high density of light-sensitive cells to let us see with higher resolution. Cell density decreases as we move away from the fovea, making our view be low definition on the sides of our visual field.

method, on the contrary, is a method of providing appropriate feedback based on the user's complete physical behavior. It is used in various forms to give realism, from a simple way of walking to a 360-degree rotation. Active methods require much more room around the user (physically) and imply the risk of injury to the user, not only by hitting furniture but also by losing equilibrium, because immersive experiences can send orientation signals to our brain different than the physical orientation of our body.

## Software for the Metaverse

To software developers, the Metaverse can be described as a combination of objects and scenes, providing an environment with content and experiences for users. Considering this approach, all software in the Metaverse can be classified into two groups: software for recognition (of objects, speech, or understanding of the environment) and software for generation (of objects, speech, or scenes).

Therefore, Metaverse applications need a step beyond conventional Internet applications, in the sense that the latter only requires recognizing where the user is pointing or clicking, while the former implies a computer *learning* and *understanding* the spatial environment of the user and his gestures. This is what is technically known as *cognition*. There are two types of cognition: static and dynamic. Static cognition is what we directly feel through senses (e.g., sight, hearing, and touch), while dynamic cognition is sensory balance and body movement. In dynamic cognition, adaptation, attention, and behavior are important features that require massive computing power.

Going further, cognition can be related to the environment or an object. As you may imagine, the cognition of an object (e.g., a ball, a car, a horse) is much easier than the cognition of the environment, which is a large combination of objects interacting with each other. The first steps of the Metaverse will imply a lot of software development for object recognition, including poses, gestures, and faces (e.g., the Apple Face ID algorithm), while environment cognition will require much more effort and is expected to come at a later stage.

Beyond conventional application software, which will be like current Internet applications, based on database management, data processing, graphical representation, and so on, we will describe in the following the genuine software that will need to be developed for the Metaverse to become a reality.

### Software for Scene and Object Recognition

Object recognition is the process of recognizing the size, shape, position, brightness, and colors of objects according to distance. Scene recognition is the recognition of the objects in a specific space surrounding the observer and the interactions between them to obtain the scene context. Scene graphs are a good approach to representing scenes so they can be interpreted by algorithms. A graph consists of nodes containing some information (e.g., the objects of the scene) and links between them, indicating interaction or relationships. **Scene graphs** are commonly used by vector-based graphics editing applications and modern computer games, which arrange the logical and often spatial representation of a graphical scene. Some techniques use generative methods and scene graphs altogether to classify objects in overlapping situations and to predict human postures based on spatial information, recorded behavior, and so on.

Again, when many objects of a scene are recognized using individual object detection, the number of computations increases in proportion to the number of objects, so sometimes some abstraction is applied to the objects to reduce the computing demand and achieve fast object recognition and efficient training. For instance, once an object is detected as a ball, to minimize the associated data to this object, it can be represented just as a sphere of a particular color, where only the coordinates of the center of the sphere, its radius, and its color are needed.

### Software for Sound and Speech Recognition

Recognizing sounds and processing speech help us understand our surroundings and communicate with others. The conversation is a direct method of communication with other people (avatars) and giving instructions to the applications in the Metaverse. There are three technologies associated with sound and speech recognition to be applied in the Metaverse:

- Noise cancellation: A technology that separates the surrounding noise and one's voice without noise.
- Spatial audio: The loudness of each sound in real life depends on distance. In the Metaverse, the same feeling must be implemented. Every sound source recorded to be used in a VR or AR environment must consider the distance and the point where the sound is coming. Thus, users will instantly know which end is the sound coming from, having a realistic, immersive experience. This is particularly relevant to providing immersive experiences in concerts and other musical events.
- Voice recognition: We are now accustomed to voice recognition, primarily because of virtual assistants like Alexa or Siri. Since the immersive experience in the Metaverse will bring extra interaction of our whole body with digital applications, voice recognition becomes essential. With time, users will demand natural interaction with realistic virtual characters in the Metaverse, sometimes very difficult to differentiate from real humans. Therefore, they will need perfect speech understanding. But much before, given that the Metaverse will provide immediateness to many aspects of our lives (e.g., traveling from one place to another in seconds, entering and leaving shops quickly) while our vision will be in the virtual world and not free to see a physical keyboard, reliable voice recognition becomes critical since the beginning.

### Software for Scene and Object Generation

The method of generating the environment and objects in the Metaverse is divided into the process of depicting by reflecting the actual world and the technique of creating a new imaginary environment. A realistic way to represent the real-world environment is to reproduce common places with high fidelity (resolution, illumination, textures, etc.), such as museums, public sites, our own home, and so on. Alternatively, it is possible to recreate hard-to-reach or completely inexistent environments like the Titanic's interiors, Moon or Mars surfaces, Star Wars Millennium Falcon, and so on, to provide a surreal experience.

But when we mention object generation, we also refer to human representations, that is, avatars. In the Metaverse, through a 3D scanner, it is possible to recreate our face and body in a perfect 3D virtual replica. ML algorithms can make the rest to simulate natural human movements on that avatar and make it see a realistic recording of ourselves. It is closely related to the concept of deepfake, which is essentially using such creation of anyone else to make others believe that something untrue was actually done or said by that person.

Finally, going deeper into the surrealistic world that the Metaverse will open, other types of objects that we already see in video games are imaginary animals (e.g., unicorns, dragons) and anthropomorphic objects (e.g., talking chairs). In conclusion, although generation in objects and scenes is initially much easier than recognition, they open an infinite world of possibilities that will make VR much richer and more exciting than the limited reality we know today.

## Software for Sound and Speech Synthesis

Sound synthesis is a field that gives the user a sense of immersion. It creates a sound in the space to provide a feeling of presence in the field and increase the sense of immersion. We differentiate two approaches:

- Speech synthesis: Much effort has been made in recent years to accomplish realistic computer speech. Some applications like Speechelo (www.speechelo.com) include intonation and accent to different voices in many languages, making it very difficult to distinguish them from actual human speech. Speech synthesis will frequently be found in many applications in such an interactive environment as the Metaverse.

- Sound synthesis: This is probably the most accessible type of development for the Metaverse, as it is already widely implemented in video games and home cinema applications. The purpose is to provide spatial audio experiences when experiencing either VR environments or AR services (e.g., traffic lights and road signals making acoustic signals to drivers only inside their cars).

### Software for Motion Rendering

There are mainly two ways to monitor users' motion and translate (render) it to the Metaverse: using cameras to record the user's poses and gestures together with image processing algorithms and providing the user with wearable devices on his legs, arms, hands, and so on to measure their position, orientation, and acceleration. While the former is less invasive and much more affordable (a simple camera and software are needed), the latter is more precise, especially under poor illumination or in places where more than one person is moving. Although today it is possible to capture the real-time 3D motion of complex scenes with a camera and isolate human body parts, this method is still limited in capturing close interactions between people (e.g., hugs) or a person and an object.

## Content as the Core of the Metaverse

Content is the fundamental component that gives sense to the Metaverse and is used to provide an immersive experience through well-organized stories and user-created events. Story reality, immersive experience, and conceptual completeness are important in content. There are two ways to create content: adapt, reuse, or produce it from scratch.

Although we are used to finding text, images, sound, and video on the Internet, it is in the Metaverse that every kind of content is brought to the next level. In the Metaverse, users create large amounts of multimedia content (e.g., images and videos) and text, not just by recording with their smartphones but primarily because they *navigate* inside a 3D virtual world composed of images, videos, and 3D objects. The multimedia data generated in this way expresses the user's thoughts and experiences and is stored and processed as *multimodal* content. Multimodal content enriches the content by adding information that can come from other elements, the environment (virtual or real), or be created by a Metaverse application using ML or similar techniques.

Additionally, since the Metaverse will contain many interconnected virtual worlds, simply connecting objects is not enough because this manual process would be unmanageable at a large scale. Thus, there is a need for a method to expand and infer links between entities according to specific rules or automation.

### Scenario Generation

A scenario is the expected journey that a user will experience when using any service in the Metaverse. Service providers must develop open and flexible scenarios that allow users to navigate—the same way as websites—but also define the ideally expected *journey* to accomplish the goals set by the service provider (e.g., buying a product, subscribing to a service, contacting a person, revealing some personal information).

For this reason, rather than listing or showing isolated events or objects in the Metaverse, it is vital to find relationships between them and construct a *scenario line* based on them. Unlike text-based scenarios or plain graphics scenarios found on websites, the Metaverse is more complex because it must be configured in multimodal and embodied environments. Entities and relationships are used to organize events, and events must be organically combined to form scenario lines. Scenario lines construct the overall structure and serve as an index linking each event.

To compose a scenario line, it is necessary to connect events consisting of entities and their relationships using a graph model. Events are divided into main events and subevents according to their relevance in the scenario's progress. Scenario construction methods include continuous sequences, hierarchical structures, and the attention-based process based on focusing on meaningful content.

When user behavior data in a scenario is accumulated over a user's avatar's lifetime, we come up with the concept of *lifelogging*; we log into the Metaverse with our "whole life" data. This creates our own *key scenario topics*, extracted with topic modeling and personalized multimodal user data. There are some examples that use lifelogging to provide maximal customization in the Metaverse, like a drama manager that personalizes user stories with plots and optimal sequences (Yu and Riedl 2012).

## Scenario Population

Scenarios expand by adding entities and linking the added entities with relations. Scenario lines form a skeleton and expand entities and links to events to create rich stories. Connections between some events and other events are formed by relationships and are linked within a scenario, forming a completely immersive user experience.

In the process of scenario graph population in the Metaverse, modal conversion (e.g., text-to-video and video-to-text conversion) is used for multimodal integration. As most of the content in the Metaverse is expected to be video, which demands a lot of computing power for processing and extracting meaning, some techniques are needed to extract valuable information in the form of text from the video sequences (e.g., the user is looking at the object, the user is picking up the object, the user stays five seconds staring at the object before touching it). This will help to build scenarios more easily as a combination of "if... then..." rules (e.g., if the user stares at the object for more than three seconds, make the object bounce and add a tag over saying "pick me").

## User-Generated Content

One of the pillars of the Metaverse is user-generated content (UGC). Like in current social media, a continuous and much richer interaction between users is expected in the Metaverse. The immersive experience it provides and the infinite possibilities to develop new applications and services will contribute to that. In this context, NFTs will provide an effective way to prove that UGC is unique and nonfungible (i.e., noninterchangeable) when this is desired. It will enable digital content owners to sell or trade their property via smart contracts.

# Summary

In this chapter, we have read about the following ideas regarding how the Metaverse is built:

- The Metaverse architecture is still under discussion. However, there is a good model proposed for the Metaverse, containing 14 elements. However, a basic approach can describe the Metaverse components in hardware, software, and content.
- The hardware is dominated by HMDs, commonly known as VR headsets. There are other devices for interacting with the Metaverse, like hand-tracking devices (based on physical controls or directly tracking hand gestures using a camera), eye tracking, wearable devices, and so on.
- Regarding software, there are different categories for the new software required in the Metaverse besides traditional applications: scene and object recognition, sound and speech recognition, scene and object generation, sound and speech synthesis, and motion rendering. There are some vendors providing the whole set (or a group of features) in a software development framework, such as Nvidia Omniverse.

# CHAPTER 6

# Immersive Technologies

## Augmented Reality, Virtual Reality, and More

The Metaverse is all about immersive experience. To make experiences immersive, virtual reality (VR), augmented reality (AR), mixed reality (MR), and extended reality (XR) are vital concepts with associated technologies. This chapter will give a practical description and some examples to illustrate how they will support the development of Metaverse applications and how they are progressing today.

## VR

VR is a concept to describe an alternative, separate environment that has been created using digital tools. This environment provides a simulated experience of a different reality and makes users feel immersed, located in a different world. VR systems operate so that the users feel "inside" another world, interacting with elements in the VR space much like in the physical world. With the help of specialized multisensory equipment such as immersion helmets, VR headsets, and omnidirectional treadmills, this experience is amplified through 3D vision, spatial sound, touch sensation, movement, and natural interaction with virtual objects. An example of VR is shown in Figure 6.1.

It can be said that VR is a computer-generated immersive three-dimensional visualization with which users can interact. VR has been in development since the 1980s. While early attempts to anticipate the uses and feel of VR may look naive and gauche in review, their tools like 3D goggles and data gloves have gradually become adopted. The opportunities

*Figure 6.1 Example of a virtual world and a person using a VR kit to move inside it handling a virtual fire extinguisher*

VR pioneers envisioned, and the aspirations of the early developers, have become part of what VR is now. For many people, the Second Life game was the first usable VR commercially available. However, back in 1994, VRML (Virtual Reality Modeling Language) was the first VR available over the Internet, allowing users to "swim through web data."

To implement VR, commercial VR headsets are equipped with sensors that detect the movement of the head (generally in three degrees of freedom, as shown in Figure 6.2).

Additionally, VR kits provide some user interaction techniques, including hand controllers. This way, users can be immersed in a virtual environment and can interact with virtual objects in a similar way to physical reality. The metaverse benefits tremendously from VR, as content and services are provided in an immersive way using VR. Nowadays, commercial virtual environments enable users to create content. Many users in such virtual environments can collaborate with each other in real time. This aligns with the well-defined requirements of the virtual environments demanded by the Metaverse: a shared sense of space, a shared sense of presence, a shared sense of time (real-time interaction), a way to

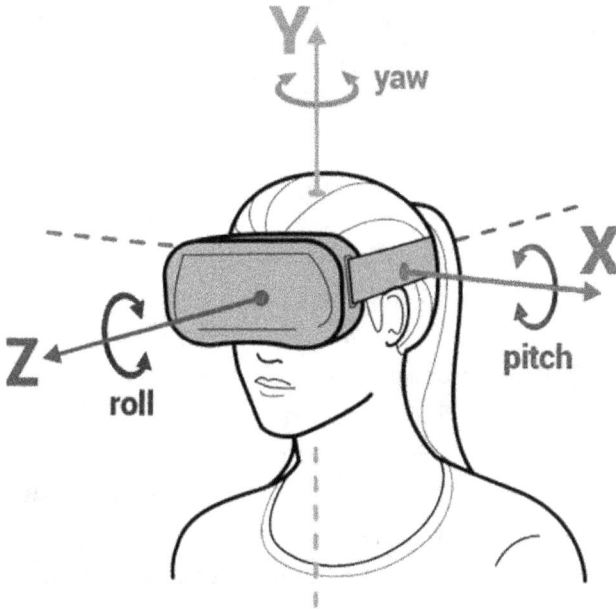

*Figure 6.2 The six degrees of freedom—two for pitch, two for roll, and two for yaw—in a VR headset*

communicate (by gesture, text, voice, etc.), and a way to share information and manipulate objects.

It can be said that VR enables virtual worlds, and virtual worlds are subsets of the Metaverse. Different users in a virtual world would receive the same information and environment. Users can also interact with each other in a consistent and real-time way. Thus, users' perception and multiuser collaboration in a virtual world are key to enabling the Metaverse experience. As we will see next, in the ultimate stage of the Metaverse, users situated in a virtual world will be able to work simultaneously not only using VR but also incorporating elements and experiences from the physical world with the help of MR and XR.

However, there is a huge challenge in combining the different VR worlds or spaces altogether to build a single Metaverse, mostly due to the inherent complexity in the design of those VR worlds and the associated high computing power. Managing and synchronizing the dynamic states and events at scale is a tremendous task, especially when we consider unlimited simultaneous users collectively acting on virtual objects and interacting with each other with low latency, that is, without perceiving a delay between the action of a user and the reaction of the virtual environment.

# AR

Following a different approach, AR embeds digital inputs and virtual elements into the physical environment. It spatially merges the physical with the virtual world. AR does not create a "virtual world" but, instead, provides additional information or adds objects to the physical world perceived by a person. This is achieved by spatially projecting a layer of digital elements on the images obtained through a camera, for example, using smartphones or tablets, or using transparent elements that can add digital representations overlapped to reality, for example, glasses, contact lenses, glass windows, or other transparent surfaces. Moreover, AR can be implemented in standard VR headsets by equipping them with pass-through mode capability that displays input from integrated camera sensors. That way, the VR headset would create a virtual world using images from the physical world in the background. An example of AR is shown in Figure 6.3.

It is said that AR provides an *enhanced* reality, although this term is subjective, and the level of this enhancement will heavily depend on the

*Figure 6.3 Example of AR providing information on local attractions over the image provided by the camera in a smartphone*

quality of the information or elements added by the AR system. Anyway, it is important to highlight that AR does not only concert visual experiences, which are, though, the most frequent. Computer-generated virtual content can be presented through other perceptual information channels, such as audio, smell, and touch (formally called "haptics"). The first generation of AR applications only considered visual enhancements, organizing and displaying digital overlays on top of the physical surroundings.

Since the very first attempts, significant research efforts have been made to improve the user interaction with digital entities in AR. It is important to note that these entities could come from the Metaverse and be overlaid in front of the user's physical surroundings. In AR, achieving low latency in the system is probably more important than in VR because part of the experience will have zero latency (the physical reality), and anything compared with something instantaneous may be perceived as a slow response. As such, guaranteeing seamless and lightweight user interaction with the digital entities in AR is one of the key challenges.

Although many smartphones already feature some AR applications, we probably imagine typical AR as the freehand interaction used in some science fiction movies like *Minority report*. In the real world, although mostly limited to research publications, there is a well-known freehand interaction technique named "Voodoo Dolls," consisting of a solution in which users can employ their two hands to choose and work on the virtual content using pinch gestures. "HOMER" is another type of user interaction solution that provides a ray-casting trajectory from a user's virtual hand, indicating the AR objects being selected and subsequently manipulated.

Regarding possible applications of AR in the Metaverse, we can figure out some of them, for instance, annotating directions in an unfamiliar place, pinpointing objects driven by the user contexts, and, in general, integrating with the urban environment. Additional information and indications will soon appear in smart cities on top of many physical objects. Even if goggles or special windshields in cars are needed, AR will let users work in the physical world while simultaneously communicating with virtual content in the Metaverse. However, this requires significant efforts in the detection and tracking technologies to map the virtual content displayed at the correct position in the real environment.

# MR

The literature also discusses about MR as a combination of VR and AR. Although there is no commonly agreed definition for MR among the scientific and technological community, it is obvious that MR refers to something between VR and AR in terms of user experience and immersion. To better comprehend the three terms and visualize how these immersive technologies interact with the environment, Milgram and Kishino's one-dimensional reality–virtuality continuum is shown in Figure 6.4. This continuum is illustrated as a straight line with two ends. On the left end, there is the natural, physical environment. The right end marks an entirely artificial, virtual environment. Hence, AR is near the left end of the spectrum while VR occupies the right extremum.

According to Lee et al. (2021), the vastly different definitions for MR can be summarized into six working definitions, including the "traditional" notion of MR in the middle space of the reality–virtuality continuum, MR as a synonym for AR, MR as a type of collaboration, MR as a combination of AR and VR, MR as an alignment of environments, and a "stronger" version of AR. Anyhow, something where anyone agrees, is that in MR, both *worlds* (virtual and physical) interact. MR is a superset of AR and VR. Some examples are a virtual switch that you can press to switch on the lights in a room physically or a virtual object or game character that can "hide" totally or partially behind physical objects (a table or a couch, for instance).

It is essential to highlight the intensive computing power required in MR to let the algorithms *understand* the environment and collect data about situational awareness. This is because, in MR, virtual objects must interact with other physical objects smoothly and seamlessly for the user. For instance, a user could use a physical screwdriver to fit and turn digital

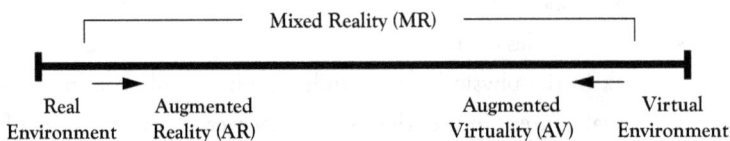

*Figure 6.4 Milgram and Kishino's one-dimensional reality–virtuality continuum*

screws in a digital 3D model of a machine, requiring that interoperability between digital and physical entities match perfectly to enjoy a realistic experience.

As shown, while AR is normally informative, adding information or objects as an overlay to physical objects or images, MR is normally used for interoperability between the user and any object (physical or digital). Considering such an additional feature, MR is viewed as a stronger or more evolved version of AR in many articles. This approach also justifies why some authors classify MR as a collaborative tool, spatial interaction between users and virtual entities.

Like in the case of VR, MR also requires special devices, normally glasses. However, the possibilities of MR go far beyond visual experience and could involve spatial audio, touching (haptics), and even smelling interaction with virtual elements when moving along physical spaces. In conclusion, MR is the starting point for the Metaverse, and certain properties of the six working definitions are commonly shared between the Metaverse and MR.

# XR

A fourth acronym related to the different levels of reality is XR, which stands for extended reality or cross reality. XR is probably the most ambiguous term in this group. It is understood as an umbrella that includes a series of immersive technologies and digital environments where data are represented and projected. Thus, XR includes VR, AR, and MR. XR can be seen as an evolution where users perceive any of the reality forms (VR, AR, or MR) with the same feeling as physical reality. Any XR user would not differentiate it from the physical reality, except for things or principles that are impossible in physical reality (e.g., a flower blossoming at a faster pace or the possibility to fly whenever desired). It can be said that XR will provide the same level of reality as dreams or illusions. Of course, this represents a technological goal that is not yet achieved by market solutions. However, some companies are doing very good progress, like Unity Technologies, Qualcomm, Oculus, Nvidia, and Steam. Some XR developments have been made for virtual commerce (or "v-commerce") to create computer-mediated indirect experiences (Alcañiz et al. 2019).

## Comparison of All Technologies

We have seen that XR is just a mature evolution of the other three technologies: VR, AR, and MR. To understand each technology with daily examples, let's show each one more graphically:

- VR can be associated with a virtual world where the user (or a user's digital avatar) directly moves or navigates. VR provides an experience as if you were in an artificial place without physical limitations.
- AR is a technology that superimposes virtual objects on real space from a first-person perspective (e.g., Pokemon Go). AR overlays computer-generated images, sounds, 3D models, videos, graphics, animated sequences, games, or GPS information into real-world environments (Oddone 2019; Townsdin and Whitmer 2017).
- MR integrates the two concepts: VR and AR. In MR applications, users interact with virtual objects projected on the physical reality.

AR provides a more realistic experience because hardware requirements are simpler, that is, glasses or a mobile device with a screen—a tablet or a smartphone–and reflects reality well, but it is suitable for less elaborated content (Alcañiz et al 2019). On the other hand, VR covers the entire field of view, provides a more immersive feeling, and is suitable for enriched content, but normally entails physical fatigue because the whole environment is new for the user and cognitive processes in the user's brain need to adapt. Additionally, VR requires a headset that isolates the user from the physical reality, which also contributes to fatigue. For these reasons, MR, which uses a mixture of the friendly physical reality and the interactive possibilities of VR, is considered as a more suitable long-term solution to experience the Metaverse.

However, it is important to separate these technologies from the concept of the Metaverse. While all of them, especially MR and XR, are enabling technologies to develop services and experiences in the Metaverse, these technologies focus on a physical approach and user experience, while the Metaverse concept also includes content and social meaning. Additionally, accessing the Metaverse does not necessarily involve the use of AR, VR, MR, or XR technologies. There could be Metaverse applications that do not use these interaction technologies. To better understand this point, we can do a comparison with the current Internet: computers' or smartphones' displays are NOT the Internet but enabling technologies to access the content and experience provided by the different services available on the Internet. Furthermore, they are not needed in all Internet services. For instance, a car can be connected to the Internet to share its location with the emergency services in the case of an accident, and no displays are involved in such services.

## Summary

In this chapter, we have learnt the differences between the different immersive technologies that enable the Metaverse. Here are the main ideas:

- Immersive technologies can be categorized into four groups: virtual reality (VR), augmented reality (AR), mixed reality (MR), and extended reality (XR).
- VR consists of creating a completely new virtual world where users navigate. They need at least VR headsets to access these worlds. The worlds can emulate physical reality (photorealistic) or be something completely different (like cartoons or even surrealistic).
- AR applications overlay digital content on pictures of physical reality. Smartphones' cameras or special transparent glasses are used to *enhance* reality with more information or objects.
- MR is a combination of VR and AR: in physical reality, some virtual objects appear using glasses or a smartphone camera. The difference with AR is that these objects can *interact* with physical reality (e.g., virtually jumping to the top of a real table or making the actual lights in the room blink each time they are virtually hit by the user).

- XR is an aspirational concept that contains all the aforementioned, where users will not differentiate what is real or virtual. For marketing purposes, many companies are using the XR term to name their VR, AR, or MR solutions, currently.

# CHAPTER 7

# Blockchain and Its Relevance for the Metaverse

Blockchain is a concept to define a distributed database in which data is stored in blocks, instead of structured tables of conventional databases. The new data stored in the database is filled into new blocks, which are linked to previous blocks, forming a *block chain*. In a blockchain database, data is thus stored in chronological order, and data in existing blocks cannot be changed. The process of storing the data in blocks is supported by a validation method based on a cryptographic function called "hash." Although it is too technical to speak about hashes here, it is important to understand that a hash is a digital code that results from applying an algorithm on a piece of data—in the case of Blockchain, a block of the chain. This code is unique, so the piece of data cannot be replaced by another or changed; otherwise, the hash would change. Thus, hash functions are used in Blockchain by the distributed nodes of the database to validate that the block that somebody is trying to add to the blockchain "matches" the rest of the chain. A high-level description of how Blockchain technology works is shown in Figure 7.1.

We mentioned previously that blockchain databases are **distributed**, which means that the database exists in many different places, simultaneously. This approach provides security in two ways:

- The stored data has **redundancy**: If some data is lost or corrupted in one instance (node) of the database, it can be recovered instantly from the other nodes.
- The stored data has **immutability**: The database can store trustworthy information, because nobody can alter the data that is already stored in a node, as the other nodes would discard the blocks that are not exact duplicates of the ones in the rest of the network.

The user requests to record an event (e.g., cryptocurrency transaction) or content (e.g., NFT)

The block is broadcasted to all nodes of the blockchain network

The block is added to the blockchain

A digital block with the event information or event is created

All nodes (consensus) or a majority validate the block according to the existing blocks in the blockchain

The user is informed about a successful record of the event or content

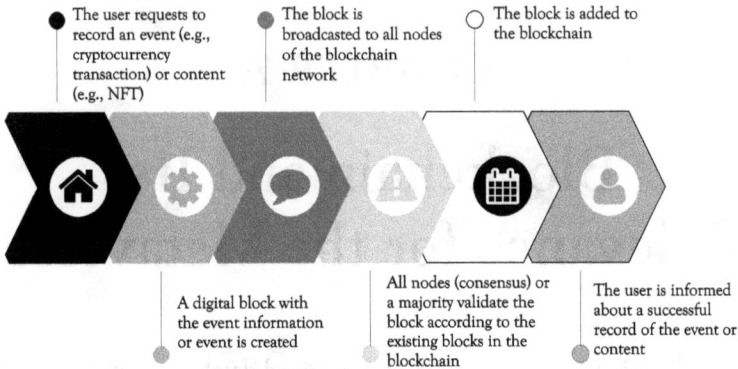

*Figure 7.1 How adding information to a blockchain works*

Under these premises, the working scheme of Blockchain technology is easily understandable: users store data in a local blockchain database node, which is synchronized with the rest of the nodes, stored in other devices, following what is called a *consensus model*. This is the main reason for using Blockchain instead of traditional databases, which have existed for decades. The problem with regular databases is that they follow the "CRUD" principle (from *Create, Read, Update, Delete*), which means you—or a hacker—can examine data, make the necessary changes, or delete information. As a result, security risks arise since there is not a constructive protection against changing or erasing data by unauthorized users.

But immutability offers more than just security. The immutability of blockchains makes them **the most transparent way to share trustworthy information** between individuals or machines. The information is extensively replicated along the planet, and anyone can read it (although there can be private blockchains, only available to a limited group of users, but this application goes beyond the purpose of this book). Transparency is another important feature for developing massive applications that rely on shared information or a common registry where all users can consult.

IBM defines a blockchain as "a shared, immutable ledger that facilitates the process of recording transactions and tracking assets in a business network." We can envisage the relevance of Blockchain from this statement: the fact that absolutely nobody can delete a bit from a block in a blockchain makes it perfect for recording transactions such as money exchange, or act as a digital registry of assets (ownership of money, real estate, academic degrees, etc.).

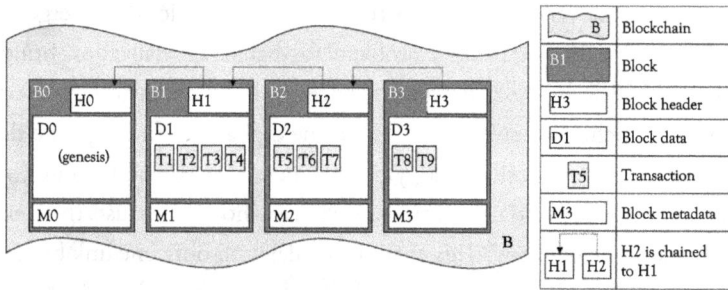

*Figure 7.2 Diagram of the block structure of a blockchain*

The typical example to illustrate Blockchain's working principle is to think of traditional accounting books, where an accountant writes new entries below the existing ones, and nothing can be deleted or modified. In fact, a blockchain is a digital ledger, where any type of data, which has been previously digitalized, can be recorded. A graphical representation of how data or events (transactions) are stored in blocks in a blockchain is shown in Figure 7.2. There, besides metadata (used to register additional information of the data stored such as the author, date, type of file, etc.), data blocks are linked by the hash information contained in their headers, as explained before.

## Blockchain Applications

Nowadays, the most popular application of Blockchain is digital currencies, or cryptocurrencies and, particularly, Bitcoin, a cryptocurrency proposed in 2009. Before going into detail about cryptocurrencies and their benefits to facilitate transactions in the fully digital world of the Metaverse, it is important to highlight that the use of Blockchain in the Metaverse, as in many other applications, goes much beyond cryptocurrencies.

Let's see some examples of how Blockchain is transforming different industries already.

### The Finance Sector

Banking was the first industry to face the threat of Bitcoin and start studying the potential applications of Blockchain. As a highly regulated sector that has traditionally operated with many players along the value chain—intermediaries—charging fees to each other, it has been a highly stable ecosystem, with very high entry barriers. In this scenario, the emergence of digital services was really a problem for banks: digitalization brings agility and flexibility (e.g., it avoids the need to handle cash and transport it to the branches or between banks) but the digital system to operate the banking industry is built like a pyramid, where "I trust you because you trust someone else who trusts someone else … who finally trusts the Central Bank of the country." This chain is fragile: with only one link broken (a bank in a default situation, a closed branch, a negative financial health evaluation from a rating agency…) can knock down the whole banking system. When Blockchain provides nearly instant financial transactions with an unbreakable technological backbone that is completely distributed and which does not need any central authority backing up the system, some reactions began.

Initially, financial institutions and governments tried to block Blockchain's emergence with regulation, but progress is hardly stoppable in the long term. Countries around the world—including the United Kingdom, Canada, Australia, and China—began investigating how they could create their own digital currencies, seizing cryptocurrency for themselves and putting money on Blockchain systems. The turning point was when they began to perceive that the benefits started outweighing the risks. Bitcoin had been able to stand up to hackers for several years, and handle the billions of transactions, demonstrating that cryptocurrency was feasible at scale.

Blockchain's adoption, mainly through cryptocurrencies, is increasing fast. Consumers can now pay friends through their phones almost instantly in almost any type of currency or cryptocurrency. More retail stores accept cryptocurrency as a payment method. El Salvador declared Bitcoin a legal national currency in the country in 2021. In Kenya, using cryptocurrency is more normal than not. However, this is still not the mainstream option for most of the world. Western markets, whose structures are mainly supported by taxes, are still immersed in how cryptocurrencies can be taxed and hinder their use while the solution to this top-priority problem arrives.

Therefore, the International Monetary Fund (IMF), the World Bank, the Bank for International Settlements, and central banks from many countries have discussed the potential uses of Blockchain technology. The first application could be facilitating bank transfers and interbank settlements, for faster and cheaper money. Another application could be the use of Blockchain to increase transparency in investment funds and derivatives, making the composition of the funds fully traceable. The ultimate application of Blockchain would be official digital currencies that citizens may use daily, but this is expected to come much later.

Another transformation that Blockchain may bring to the finance sector is related to microinvestments and microcredits. They will be an attractive outlet enabled globally and locally through Blockchain trading platforms. Using Blockchain technology will also give them the means of investing in companies and their specific activities with agility, flexibility, and without intermediaries that take a percentage of the investment. These services are currently being provided by some marketplaces or portals, called decentralized autonomous organizations (DAOs).

As an additional application, credit card companies may use Blockchain to settle the transaction, reduce fraud, and lower their own costs. This is directly related to the concept of "micropayment," which is largely strengthened by Blockchain technology. While some early initiatives are currently available, fraud rates and manageability at a large scale are two challenges that will be only solved by the implementation of Blockchain.

But let's think about the broader impacts of Blockchain technology on the global economy. The increased trust and traceability inherent to this technology could help integrate poorer and less developed countries' economies into the global financial ecosystem. As a result, they will become wealthier and, subsequently, the cost of commodities and labor may increase. Another broader impact of Blockchain application in the financial ecosystem is the overall fraud reduction and the increase of compliance with rules and regulation. Instead of using audit for postmortem analyses of fraudulent situations, record systems that have Blockchain technology integrated within them will be able to audit a file as it is created, flagging incomplete or unusual files as they are created. Besides having exhaustive audits in real time, this will give managers the tools they need to proactively correct files before they become a problem.

### The Real Estate Sector

Real estate will be one of the industries most impacted by innovations in Blockchain technology, although the impact will be different in every country. For instance, in the western world, we might see things like transparent mortgage-backed securities traded on Blockchain-enabled exchanges. In China, Blockchain integration in the real-estate value chain is already in place with things like notarization, an essential component of real estate transactions. In the developing world, Blockchain represents a great promise because it may help in freeing capital and increasing trade.

A specific transformation that Blockchain will bring to real estate is the theoretical elimination of title insurance. Title insurance provides compensation for financial loss from defects in a title for a real estate purchase. It is required if a mortgage is taken out on a home or if it is refinanced. Title insurance protects the bank's investment against eventual title problems that might not be found in the public records, are missed in the title search, or occur from fraud or forgery. Blockchain technology has been proposed as a supplement to help consumers in common law title systems. The idea is simple: Blockchains are fantastic public recordkeeping systems; they also cannot be backdated or changed without a record.

In fact, one of the largest costs associated with mortgages comes years after the loan was first made. Frequently, many documents—even some unnecessary ones—are filed together in the mortgage file. Also, duplicate records may occur. When, for any reason, there is a need to audit the file, there is too much information to sift through, which costs a lot of money. Blockchain would not only avoid this situation by storing just the essential information without any duplicate or inconsistency but also change the need for central repositories for files. It would automate some of the processing of the paperwork and would always give a clear history of the loan, reducing the need to audit and prepare documents to be verified.

### The Insurance Sector

The impact on the insurance sector will be mostly associated with the use of smart contracts, which will be described in detail in Chapter 9. These contracts heavily rely on the use of the **Internet of Things (IoT)**, which is the term to describe the plethora of digital devices that are connected to the Internet and operate autonomously. Some examples are traffic lights, surveillance cameras, weather stations, pollution sensors, cleaning robots, and so on. IoT devices can publish all kinds of data autonomously to their records and update the current state they are in. This fact makes it possible for insurance smart contracts to use this data to verify if certain conditions are met and launch automatic actions, accordingly.

IoT will likely have a significant impact on three areas: the connected car, the connected home, and the connected *self*. IoT is a disruptive technology and, as such, it will change the shape of a broad range of industries, such as automotive original equipment manufacturers (OEMs), home security, and cable and mobile providers. Insurance companies are closely connected to them, particularly the ones that work with property and casualty (P&C) policies. The data gathered by the sensors in new appliances and devices, along with the automation and additional control options, combined with Blockchain's decentralized ledgers and smart contracts, will bring the risk calculation and the overall automation in the insuring procedure to a level that has been impossible before.

Because Blockchain brings transparency to all its applications, it is perfect to be used in contracts, combined with IoT devices, especially in those small contracts related to specific things. While signing traditional contracts for such things—like an insurance contract for a flight ticket—could be lengthy, expensive, or even unfeasible, Blockchain allows full integration and real-time celebration of contracts in the digital space. It will be possible to create marketplace platforms that insure customers, for example. With this type of model, the insurer could calculate the premium for the specific risk, based on specific, actual historical data and other risk factors, in a fully automated way. This new insurance model could be adopted by peer-to-peer (P2P, when one individual insures another using a marketplace as the negotiation space), crowd-funded insurance (when individuals participate collectively in an insurance policy using a crowdfunding platform), or a traditional insurance company that adopts the technology. Either way, all are created in a decentralized blockchain with the use of smart contracts, which guarantee the payment from the customer to the insurer and vice versa if the risk materializes.

Additionally, the self-executing nature of smart contracts that will be described in Chapter 9 will cut many of the costs of claims associated with insurance and current third-party costs of intermediaries that help with the processing and collection of funds.

But, if anything is going to change the insurance sector for good, that is microinsurance. Microinsurance is insurance to protect low-value items or low-income people against risks, such as accidents, illness, and natural disasters. It has become more feasible through Blockchain technology. Microinsurance is categorized into two groups: (1) insurance targeted to low-income households, farmers, and other entities where the insurance is designed around specific needs—typically, a low-premium and index-based insurance and (2) insurance that deals with low-value products or services.

The biggest issue with these types of contracts within traditional insurance models is that their handling costs are disproportionately high compared to their small premiums. The key advantage of Blockchain is that the creation of smart contracts associated with microinsurance allows for secure transactions without any middleman, so it has significantly lower costs.

Besides this ease of use, smart contracts allow for index-based insurance, which is very useful for agricultural insurance and other fields where the values depend greatly on dynamic factors that can be accurately documented by trusted third parties. In this case, insured farmers can receive automated payouts when some conditions, such as drought, are reported by verified meteorological databases, thus further reducing potential service costs.

## The Government

When speaking about Blockchain used in governmental institutions, the first concept that arises is "**smart city**." Smart cities are urban areas that use different digital technologies and sensors to monitor and measure local events and collect data that is further analyzed and used either to make governmental decisions or to automatically activate alerts, manage resources, or adapt services to make them more efficient or to improve the well-being of the citizens in that area. Some examples of services improved by the application of digital technologies in smart cities are traffic and transportation systems, power plants, utilities, water supply networks, waste, crime detection, information systems, schools, libraries, hospitals, and other community services. Smart cities are taking advantage of modern technology to enhance infrastructure function, and safety, besides improving public services. The business of becoming a smart city is booming, and almost every larger municipality has embraced the smart city concept.

Blockchain is especially useful when integrated with the IoT used in smart cities. Many interesting projects are being accomplished and planned for the next years. Blockchain technology can be used to securely share information between networks in a smart city. Many cities are exploring how to use Blockchain to alleviate traffic jams. Singapore's Smart Nation project is exploring, among many other things, how to use the mobile phones of its citizens to measure the conditions of their bus rides, and then analyze the data to see when roads need to be upgraded. Singapore has been a leader in smart city development and has become an advisor and reference for developing smart cities in other countries.

Besides smart cities, Blockchain has many other uses in governmental ecosystems. In health care systems, it can help in digitizing patients' records and storing them in a blockchain to have full traceability—and data privacy—of patients' histories. There are also some initiatives related to high-value asset transmission such as gold or diamonds, where traditional certificates are substituted by records in a blockchain that cannot be forged or lost. Even some initiatives use Blockchain for business registration, to incentivize tourism through loyalty points programs based on smart contracts that check when a tourist visits certain attractions, and so on.

But, on the other side, we find governments normally reluctant to accept the most prominent use of Blockchain: cryptocurrencies. Either there is no regulation or there is a regulation *against* them in most of the countries. As mentioned before, the fear of having something so disruptive out of the established financial ecosystem and, furthermore, potentially out of the scope of taxation, is a major setback. And this, sometimes, makes politicians reluctant toward Blockchain technology in general, not just cryptocurrencies.

# Conclusion

Once the Metaverse is mature, it is expected that almost everything in the physical world will be connected to the digital reality of the Metaverse. Everything will be digitized, including *digital twins* for physical entities and systems (discussed in Chapter 16), avatars for users, large-scale, fine-grained maps, and so on. As a result, a huge amount of data will be generated. Uploading such giant data to centralized cloud servers is impossible, due to the limited network resources, but it is possible to apply Blockchain to decentralized data storage systems to guarantee consistency and security of that data in the Metaverse.

# Summary

This chapter has introduced Blockchain technology and its potential applications. We have read about the following ideas:

- Blockchain technology is an innovative way to store data in a decentralized and secure way. The methods used guarantee trust and preservation of the data.
- There is no authority on any blockchain, all nodes operate collaboratively to validate new data entries.
- Data cannot be changed or deleted from a blockchain. Everything is stored for good. This is part of the reason why they are trustworthy.
- In the finance industry, Blockchain has its primary application in the production of cryptocurrency.
- There are other sectors where Blockchain brings substantial improvements, like real estate and insurance, thanks to the use of smart contracts.
- Smart cities can also benefit from Blockchain technology by adding more services to the current portfolio (e.g., fostering IoT data, integrating health care applications).

# CHAPTER 8

# The Relationship Between the Metaverse and Cryptocurrencies

Before going into detail about how cryptocurrencies may benefit the adoption of the Metaverse, it is important to perfectly understand what cryptocurrencies are. To understand cryptocurrencies, we must first remember how traditional currencies work.

## The Money System

The amount of available money is controlled by central banks. The issuance or potential destruction of U.S. dollars is made exclusively by the Federal Reserve System. The same happens for euros and the European Central Bank, and so with all other currencies on Earth. One of the top priorities of a central bank is to keep money value in a certain range, normally assuming a depreciation target of around 2 percent each year (which is called *inflation* of the economy). They can work toward this goal by printing more banknotes, changing interest rates of the issuance of debt to regular banks, setting reserve requirements, and so on.

This method follows a simple economic principle: if there is a scarcity of a commodity, its value goes up. If it is abundant, its value goes down. To stabilize the value of a currency, seeking a low value for inflation—2 percent—central banks tweak money distribution on a regular basis.

At this point, you may agree that money's actual value is "what it is," I mean, all citizens have faith in a currency's value to purchase things. This is the reason why traditional currencies are called *fiat* money (*fiat* means "be done" in Latin). In fact, money has no *real* value, it only has *attributed* value since governments declare it legal tender, essentially making it debt.

If a central bank *decides* that its currency is worth half its value, or one-tenth its value, *so be it.*

## The Cryptocurrency Pattern

Cryptocurrencies were built differently. You may have heard about the *gold pattern.* In the past, money was only an easier form of exchange than trading with physical gold in regular transactions. Instead of giving half an ounce of gold, you delivered a banknote, issued, and certified by the national central bank, confirming that this banknote gave the other party the right to claim a specific amount of gold from the national gold reserve. Previously, of course, you had to deposit that amount of gold in the reserve to obtain that banknote. Gold, like silver, platinum, and other precious metals, was considered valuable because it is finite, scarce, and preserves its value over time (precious metals do not rust). It is a tangible, limited asset but, again, its value is given by the market, that is, people. Cryptocurrencies are much like virtual gold.

Using Blockchain technology, most cryptocurrencies are designed to be finite. Bitcoin, for example, has a limited supply of 21 million. The same as gold, cryptocurrencies are finite and scarce assets, but they are virtual instead of physical. This, in fact, is an advantage because it is much easier to trade with cryptocurrencies than with gold, and cryptocurrencies are much easier to protect and store. However, to become a currency, anything claimed so must be assigned a value by the market (people). In the last decade, this barrier was broken due to their efficiency as a trade medium and the need for the increasing generation of billionaires to diversify their assets. Thus, do not be fooled: any cryptocurrency has value because there is a community of billionaires—the same than invest in the stock market—trusting them. Even though they may suffer enormous fluctuation until reaching maturity, they will continue existing for a very long time. And the Metaverse is going to actively contribute to that.

## Cryptocurrencies in the Metaverse

Everything must be digital in the Metaverse, by design. Thus, payments must be done with digital currencies. Although today all banks use electronic transactions and payments, there is a tremendous risk in the global banking system: in theory, all electronic transactions should have a physical asset—even under the weak form of a banknote—to support that transaction. But there is a trick called debt, which allows new money not backed by any physical asset. Debt is money *coming from the future*. That said, most of the actual money is not real and it only exists in a digital registry in a bank. If the supporting systems—which use traditional databases—are hacked or data is lost, the money is gone. Therefore, the Blockchain technology is essential, and this is the reason why large economic powers like China have launched their current version of their currencies (e.g., the *e-Yuan*) or, like the European Union, are preparing their future launch or, like the United States, are studying the potential impacts of doing so.

A *digital currency* and a *cryptocurrency* are essentially the same. The only difference between them is that the latter is not associated with any country or central bank, while the former is controlled by them. Regarding their use in the Metaverse, everything is to be made yet but, like in our current world, an active presence is expected of both forms of Blockchain-based money. Therefore, knowledge of ***virtual currencies*** (the concept to name digital currencies and cryptocurrencies altogether) is highly useful to your business or the investment you intend to make in the next years. Although there are more than 10,000 active ones at the moment of writing this book (Table 8.1), most of them will die sooner than later, as always happens to new, emerging markets (in fact, nearly 20,000 were created in total). In a virtual currency, it is essential to understand where its value relies on, and who its major holders are.

## The Current Landscape of Cryptocurrencies for the Metaverse

There are some cryptocurrencies currently operating solutions in the second iteration of the Metaverse, as seen in Chapter 1. There are many 3D immersive worlds in existence today, mostly associated with video games, as discussed in Chapter 2. Many of these games and services allow users to purchase digital items such as outfits and accessories to customize the players' in-game look or improve their avatars' performance.

*Table 8.1  Evolution of cryptocurrencies*

| Year | Number of Cryptocurrencies |
|------|---------------------------|
| 2013 | 7 |
| 2014 | 67 |
| 2015 | 501 |
| 2016 | 572 |
| 2017 | 636 |
| 2018 | 1,359 |
| 2019 | 2,086 |
| 2020 | 2,403 |
| 2021 | 4,154 |
| 2022 | 10,363 |

*Table 8.2  The market capitalization of Metaverse cryptocurrencies above $150 million by the end of the first half of 2022*

| Cryptocurrency | Related application | Market capitalization |
|----------------|---------------------|-----------------------|
| MANA | Decentraland | $1.86B |
| SAND | The Sandbox | $1.62B |
| THETA | Theta Network | $1.44B |
| AXS | Axie Infinity | $1.43B |
| ENJ | Enjin Coin | $520M |
| WEMIX | WEMIX | $348M |
| ONT | Ontology | $216M |
| WAXP | WAX | $215M |
| CEEK | CEEK VR | $188M |
| PLA | PlayDapp | $171M |
| SUSHI | SushiSwap | $159M |

Consequently, the list of cryptocurrencies related to Metaverse applications with a market capitalization above 150 million U.S. dollars by the end of the first half of 2022, shown in Table 8.2, is dominated by games.

Although cryptocurrencies in Metaverse applications are used to purchase items, services, or features in their respective apps—even when some cryptocurrencies are accepted in more than one game or application—sometimes they are called **crypto-tokens** as their main purpose is not trading with them in the markets but be used as virtual assets inside the game.

The main problem associated with these cryptocurrencies is that their values are extremely volatile, much more than that of general-purpose cryptocurrencies like Bitcoin or Ether. The reason behind that is that they not only depend on the dynamics of the cryptocurrency market (sometimes abbreviated as the "crypto market") but also on the popularity of their respective game or even on the possibilities or new features this game allows for the crypto-token. A brief review of the most relevant ones is provided in the following.

### MANA (by Decentraland)

Although Decentraland has been already mentioned in Chapter 4, when speaking of the most important initiatives in the Metaverse by American companies, we will see more details about this platform in Chapter 12. It is a metaverse platform where users can develop and monetize content and apps in 3D virtual spaces. MANA, Decentraland's official cryptocurrency, is built on the Ethereum blockchain and allows users to acquire or exchange land in this virtual world, as well as pay for products and services in that environment, such as estates, avatars, wearables, and unique names on the platform's marketplace. It is a finite cryptocurrency, like Bitcoin, and there is a total of 2.19 billion MANA tokens available for purchase.

### SAND (by the Sandbox)

The Sandbox was briefly mentioned in Chapter 2 and will be further detailed in Chapter 12. Basically, it is a platform that integrates blockchain, cryptocurrencies, and NFTs into a 3D metaverse. With the use of free creative tools, its virtual environment enables players to develop and personalize their own games and digital assets for commercialization as NFTs on the platform's marketplace, where other users can use SAND tokens (or SAND *virtual coins*, to better understand this concept) to pay.

Additionally, SAND holders may earn prizes, which includes a share of the profit generated by all SAND transactions. Having SAND tokens also increases the likelihood of discovering "precious gems" and "catalysts" required to create rare assets on the platform. One characteristic of the

SAND cryptocurrency is that it is not only available in The Sandbox game but also in cryptocurrency exchange markets, like the famous portal Binance.

### THETA *(by the Theta Network)*

THETA token went live in 2019, by a group of entrepreneurs in Silicon Valley. The venture is supported by corporate investors like Sierra Ventures, Sony Innovation Fund, Samsung, and some others. The Theta Network is not a game but a decentralized video content streaming platform, powered by users and an innovative new blockchain. The initiative counts on renowned advisors such as Steven Chen Shijun, cofounder of YouTube, and Justin Kan, cofounder of Twitch.

The Theta Network utilizes an open-source protocol that is specifically designed to decentralize streaming services. The unique nature of the Theta Network blockchain will also allow for the creation of decentralized app layers that provide specific functions, such as peer-to-peer streaming, live sports broadcasts, education, conferencing, television, and movies.

Although the initiative is still in an early stage, it is expected that people will utilize THETA tokens as a method for paying and renumerating content creators, trading virtual products and buying premium services.

### AXS *(by Axie Infinity)*

Axie Infinity is a game about breeding, growing, and combating virtual creatures known as Axies. In 2018, Sky Mavis developed the platform, which reached around 2.7 million daily active users in 2021. Axies creatures and virtual real estate are sold using NFTs on this game's marketplace, with most transactions taking place on a simplified version of the Ethereum blockchain called "Ronin" (less secure, but with lower transaction fees also).

Axie Infinity defines itself as a play-to-earn game, where players can sell items through the game's marketplace as well as receive tokens from the game. So, once you feed and train your Axie properly, its value increases, and you will be able to sell it for a higher price than the one you paid for it. Like in The Sandbox, this game also allows users to purchase and sell AXS tokens on cryptocurrency exchange markets such as Coinbase.

### ENJ or "Enjin coin" (by Enjin)

Enjin is a platform for creating online gaming communities. Its mission is to simplify gaming by delivering cryptocurrency-backed tools, which include game plugins, software development kits (SDKs), and virtual item management applications, all of them set as NFTs in the platform. Enjin also provides cryptocurrency related features like wallets and a payment gateway platform. It uses the Ethereum blockchain and, when a new NFT is created on the system, its value—in ENJ—is set in a smart contract.

### SUSHI (by SushiSwap)

SushiSwap is home to a popular decentralized exchange that allows users to buy and sell digital currencies. To enter the Metaverse, the company built an NFT marketplace called "The Shoyu," which lets digital artists producing NFTs implement 3D galleries in the platform, that also counts on a virtual "sushi bar" to enable collectors and creators to interact with each other by chatting.

In The Shoyu, collectors can also purchase links for their own NFT galleries, which can be customized as they see fit. These links will be visited by other people and will provide a better way of displaying virtual art—NFT—collections.

## The Future of Cryptocurrency and the Metaverse

We have seen that the Metaverse and cryptocurrency are concepts that go hand-in-hand: virtual worlds and virtual money to spend in them. However, the Metaverse and cryptocurrency are separate concepts and can perfectly exist without each other, at least for the moment.

However, it is clear that there is a potential synergy between the two ideas, and they will converge in time. As soon as the Metaverse offers valuable items, even virtual ones, people will demand easy, fast, and trust-able payment methods, and cryptocurrencies are the best solution for such fully digital worlds.

It is also interesting that given the huge potential the Metaverse offers to transform businesses, people, and society in general, it has the potential to significantly impact the way cryptocurrencies evolve, and the impact they will eventually have on society as well.

### The Power of Simplification

One of the big advantages of the Metaverse is that there is a lot less friction than in the physical world. In the Metaverse, if we want to go somewhere, we simply click a link, say an order, or do a gesture, and we are there. There is no need for costly and cumbersome transport infrastructure, energy and time consumption, bureaucracy, or luggage packing.

As we saw in the beginning of this chapter, the same is true of cryptocurrencies. Transacting in traditional money—fiat currencies—requires a vast infrastructure of banks and regulators to act as custodians, intermediaries, and clearinghouses. Transacting in cryptocurrencies, on the other hand, generally just requires software running on standard computers or smartphones.

As the Metaverse becomes more popular, and more of our lives are spent online, working in virtual offices, playing video games with our friends, or even taking Metaverse vacations, we will need seamless ways to pay for virtual goods and services. Even they could be for buying virtual real estate, if we want to own our own slice of digital land on which to entertain friends or start a business.

In fact, the Metaverse could add significant value to the global economy—according to McKinsey in 2022, it could reach $5 trillion by 2030. And much of that value is expected to be realized in cryptocurrency. This could mean cryptocurrency truly breaking into the mainstream as more and more people become familiar to using them as a means of payment.

When this happens, then governments and legislators will undoubtedly feel the need to step up efforts to regulate and control cryptocurrencies. As we have already mentioned, it will surely boost the emergence of "official" cryptocurrencies for some regions, like the already existing e-Yuan and the "digital euro," currently under study. In the meantime, regarding currently available cryptocurrencies, although things have become more organized in recent years—with a growing number of countries beginning to introduce regulatory frameworks around digital currency—there is still a lot to do regarding governance and other organizational aspects in this field. This translates into little protection for buyers or businesses that rely on cryptocurrencies like Bitcoin, Litecoin, or Dogecoin to do business now and little recourse for consumers, should they fall victim to the large number of scams that are out there.

As it becomes more popular, governments could also choose to regulate cryptocurrencies according to how energy-efficient or polluting they are. For example, networks that rely on more energy-demanding algorithms could be imposed with higher tax rates on transactions, while those that use the more efficient algorithms could be taxed at a lower rate.

### The Next Steps

As cryptocurrency becomes the main medium of exchange for people buying and selling in the Metaverse, its users will become increasingly comfortable with methods of acquiring, handling, and storing it. This means it will be more frequently used outside of the Metaverse, too, like for sending money to friends and family, for example. This will be particularly important if these exchanges involve the money crossing national borders, which, with regular currency, often incur heavy fees.

This, in turn, means that banks and other existing financial institutions will be likely to step up their efforts to facilitate cryptocurrency or blockchain-derived financial models. In fact, this is already happening now. To remain competitive in an age of borderless, middleman-free financial systems powered by modern fintech companies, all financial institutions, especially banks, need to streamline their own infrastructure. While some experts foresee that cryptocurrency could eventually spell the end of banking as we know it, in the near term, it is more likely that people and businesses will still want to benefit from the layer of protection and regulation that banks and central banks bring to transactional networks. But the ones that thrive in this new environment of digital currencies and peer-to-peer finance will be those that are flexible and forward-looking with their own policies when it comes to cryptocurrency adoption. PayPal and Mastercard are examples of payment systems that are fully engaging with cryptocurrency (Bitcoin in particular), and both have said it is because they believe that cryptocurrency will play an important role in the future of payments.

In conclusion, when it comes to establishing the currency of the Metaverse, cryptocurrencies are clearly the most natural fit. As both technologies are still emerging and in a very early state, it is expected that each one will influence in the development of the other. And also, their evolutionary courses are likely to be influenced by changes in the way society experiences the new digital reality. It is true that more people spend more of their time online, and this will increase as the online world becomes more immersive, entertaining, and engaging with the upcoming Metaverse. A consequence is that cryptocurrencies will play a bigger role in our lives.

## Summary

In this chapter, we have reviewed how cryptocurrencies work and some ideas about their expected impact on the Metaverse, as follows:

- The current fiat money system is based on trusting central banks to produce money at controlled pace to keep more or less its value. Cryptocurrencies use Blockchain-based algorithms to record transactions and can provide a limited number of tokens ("virtual coins") to make them valuable.
- Although very few cryptocurrencies are as famous as Bitcoin or Ether, there are a lot—over 10,000. New cryptocurrencies are launched every day. However, most of them only survive months, days, or even hours before losing their value and disappearing.
- Some of the existing cryptocurrencies are directly associated to Metaverse applications or games or can be used within them. The most popular are MANA (used in Decentraland), SAND (in The Sandbox), THETA (developed by the Theta Network), AXS (used in the Axie Infinity game), ENJ (used in Enjin), and SUSHI (by SushiSwap).
- Cryptocurrencies and the Metaverse will converge soon. The simplified and frictionless environment provided by VR and the large number of applications developed for the Metaverse will attract money and transactions, and cryptocurrencies are the perfect match—simple and capable of operating complex transactions at large scope.

# CHAPTER 9

# Smart Contracts and NFTs

## Ownership and Interaction in the Metaverse

NFT is an acronym widely found on the news. As we will see later, an NFT, which stands for "Nonfungible Token," is a piece of software that uses a blockchain to certify with total guarantee that a digital asset (a file) is unique and associated to a specific owner. As we will see in this chapter, this is crucial to allow transactions of virtual objects in the Metaverse. Eventually, some virtual objects could be bidirectionally linked to their physical counterparts, making NFTs a valuable element to protect private property in general.

NFTs are based on the technology of smart contracts. As we see next, smart contracts are related to interactions, not only in the digital world but also in our daily lives. They increase the level of confidence in contracts by automating contract execution when the conditions set are met and providing total trust through making contracts be "engraved on stone"—better said in our times, registered in a blockchain.

## What Are Smart Contracts

A smart contract is a contract that is associated, intrinsically and inseparably, with a small computer application that makes use of blockchain technology to fulfill **three functions**:

1. Attest and record without a doubt the existence and terms of the contract;

2. Verify in real time the fulfillment or not of the different clauses of the contract; and

3. Launch the appropriate actions included in the contract, according to the fulfillment or not of each clause.

As we can see, a smart contract could be defined as an "automatic execution" contract between the parties, in the sense that it is not necessary for any of them, nor any third party or commission, to watch the contract fulfillment or not to initiate the consequences. All parties who signed the contract will be aware of the outcome immediately.

The **direct implications** of smart contracts are enormous:

- No third party is needed—a notary, arbitrator, or similar—to attest the contract. The contract is maintained as if it were a private contract but, as it is protected by the blockchain network, it can be used as irrefutable proof if necessary. Even this, as we will see in the following, will not be necessary either.

- The clauses are always respected, whether what they stipulate is fulfilled, since the computer application inevitably launches the actions without anything or anyone being able to prevent it. The piece of software that contains the smart contract conditions is attached to the selected blockchain and distributed around the world, so nobody can ever change it.

- Any compensation or claim mechanism in the contract, in addition to being launched automatically, may be immediate (or not, depending on the terms agreed in the contract).

- When signing a smart contract, respecting the law becomes essential, since it will be impossible to block the execution of automatic actions once the contract is registered in the blockchain, even if they conflict with the law. Anything illegal in the contract could only be claimed a posteriori once the automated actions have been executed.

Smart contracts can be used for anything and, in the future, we will surely carry out real estate sales and the issuance of academic titles through this means. However, the first steps in smart contracts are being taken in contracts with a smaller scope such as, for instance, the delivery of goods. If you have ever bought online, you will have seen that you must first pay for the merchandise, and then it arrives at your home. It is necessary to make a leap of faith that everything will work out as expected, but the chain could fail at any point, intentionally or unintentionally (the online store could be a scam and do not ship any product, the product could be out of stock and the company leave you waiting during weeks even if they promised fast delivery, the logistics operator could lose or break the product, the carrier could leave it to a neighbor who does not warn you, etc.).

With a smart contract, the entire value chain becomes trustworthy: instead of paying for the merchandise, you sign an agreement in which, when the product effectively reaches your hands, a payment will be made from your card to the seller. This will be verified because the package itself will have an RFID tag incorporated (the same one that is attached to clothes in stores and makes the alarm sound when you leave the store without paying). The logistics operator will read that label when picking up the merchandise and you will also read it with your mobile when the courier delivers it to you. Possibly, the box will also incorporate an impact sensor so that, when making the delivery, it is instantly communicated whether the package has suffered a severe impact and, instantly, the courier's terminal will not allow the delivery, you and the seller will receive a warning and, automatically, the logistics operator will compensate the seller according to the agreed terms.

All this, which seems quite complex and almost science fiction, can be assimilated much more easily if you search RFID readers or impact sensors on the Internet and realize that they sell for less than a dime. The technology is already available; it is only a matter of time before we will see it spread to all aspects of our lives.

## Benefits of Smart Contracts

Figure 9.1 summarizes the benefits provided by smart contracts:

- **Security**: All the terms of the contract are collected in a blockchain system that makes it always available and

*Figure 9.1  The benefits of smart contracts*

distributed throughout the network. It is impossible for the contract to be "lost."

- **Precision**: As its terms are codified by means of a small piece of software (called a script), the conditions that allow determining whether each clause is fulfilled or not must always be absolutely precise, otherwise, they would not be transferable to computer language.

- **Quick execution**: Like any digital service, a smart contract runs on computer systems almost instantly. It is not necessary to carry out any additional manual procedure or wait to see if a condition is met or not.

- **Cost-effective**: By eliminating actors (mainly third parties, such as notaries and even the judicial system, initially), it is the most economical solution for trustworthy agreements, especially between distant or unknown parties where, frequently, the judicial system tends to fail or be extraordinarily expensive.

- **Total trust**: Since all the terms and actions are stored in a blockchain system, neither party needs to have faith in any matter. Once signed, the contract will be executed irremediably, with the only exception that the Internet disappears from Earth.

- **Interruption-free**: As mentioned, nothing can stop a smart contract from running to completion. Neither the parts nor external phenomena can interrupt its execution.
- **Autonomy**: Once signed, a smart contract will function as an independent entity from the parties. Even if one of the parties disappears, the contract will remain.

## How Does a Smart Contract Work?

Figure 9.2 shows the steps to carry out a smart contract in a good or service sale operation. The smart contract completely replaces the traditional written contract. One of the differences between smart contracts and traditional contracts is that not only the buyer and the seller have an active role in the contract but also the asset (the good or service that is being traded). On the contrary, in traditional contracts, the asset has a merely passive role. This is so because, depending on the fulfillment or not of the different clauses of the contract ("terms & conditions"), the asset will act in a certain way or another. Thus, the smart contract is self-executing, that is, the algorithm it implements will always verify compliance with the clauses and *inform* the asset on how to proceed. In the simplest case, if the payment of a good is confirmed, the delivery order will be automatically given. In other more complex cases, penalties could be established, for example, or even a formal notice issued to a third party to report an irregularity or the intention to start a lawsuit.

We have seen the *theoretical operation* of the smart contract, which is quite simple. However, its practical implementation entails considerably more complexity. There are two fundamental challenges to solve, as follows:

- It is extremely important that the clauses of the contract are correctly programmed in the smart contract so that there are no errors in its interpretation and execution. Numerous surveys, carried out on all kinds of profiles of people, show greater confidence in machines than in people themselves. However, technology fails more and more, mainly due to the progressive increase in the complexity of systems. This makes

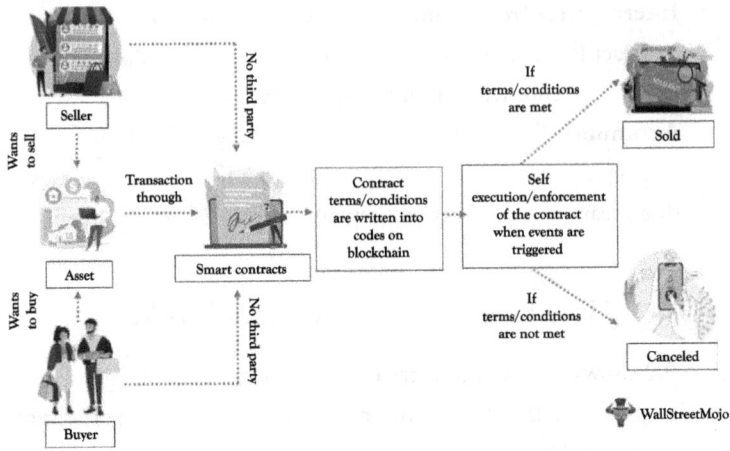

*Figure 9.2 Workflow to sign and execute a smart contract in a commercial transaction*

it impossible to control what is technically called "error states" (informally, an error state is where an algorithm could end up if any of the variables involved do not have a value considered *normal* … Remember the classical Windows blue screens, for example). Therefore, it is very important that the algorithm that implements the smart contract has sufficient robustness, which is directly related to its simplicity.

• For a smart contract to be able to make automatic decisions on compliance or not with the clauses it contains, it must have access to information on certain environmental variables. It could be said that it needs *eyes* to *see* what is happening and then determine the next actions. Since a smart contract is an algorithm—digital by nature—it is necessary that all this information reaches the system that contains the algorithm in digital form. This translates into the need to place digital sensors able to continuously measure certain variables. In the case of the transport of fresh or frozen food, for instance, it may be essential in the contract to preserve the cold chain, so a digital temperature sensor will be needed. In other cases, for example in a transaction with different currencies involved, a connector with the exchange rate information systems will be necessary. In other *exotic* arrangements, for example a smart contract to hire a "dog walker" (so famous in New York City), it would be convenient for the dog to wear a GPS collar. And, without thinking about such bizarre cases, a smart contract for roadside assistance should have a fairly large set of sensors in a vehicle to automatically call the emergency services and report whether passengers are conscious or not, what impact type and force the vehicle has suffered, if there is a risk of fire due to fuel spill, if the vehicle stays on or off the road, if it is upside down, and so on. With this example, we can realize one of the greatest advantages of smart contracts compared to simply using a private system without generally accepted and tested protection against fraud: with smart contracts implemented in vehicles, they could automatically *warn* the road signals, the emergency services, and the rest of the vehicles to take specific actions (e.g., block a lane or an entire section of the road, temporarily reduce the speed limit, etc.).

In conclusion, smart contracts will progressively conquer more different sectors. The enormous proliferation of digital sensors at a very low cost, because of their use in the smartphone industry, will help to speed up the adoption. Regarding Blockchain supporting technology, today, the Ethereum network is widely adopted, as it was the first to offer smart contract implementation.

## Important Questions About Smart Contracts

To conclude, the three probably most relevant issues to consider in the use of smart contracts are as follows:

- **Define the terms very well**: The clauses of the contract are monitored in real time by the blockchain network and automatic actions are executed, without human intervention, accordingly. Thus, it is essential that all the terms are perfectly described in the clauses of the contract. Owing to their building technique (an algorithm), smart contracts do not allow gaps or inconsistencies in their terms. They work in a purely logical way, with clauses of the type "If ... then ...." It is, therefore, necessary to define smart contracts as we code algorithms. Perhaps we will see, shortly, *software development lawyers* and law firms with a significant team of software developers.

- **Respect the law**: A smart contract does not *know* the law. We all know that laws take precedence over contracts, but this issue is normally settled by a judge or arbitrator. Although a smart contract could be claimed in court, its objective is precisely to avoid that by making an autonomous and trustworthy agreement between the parties. For this reason, while the legislation of a country is not expressed in rules *understandable* by smart contracts, it is possible that some contract violates the law. This is not different from what happens today with regular contracts, but we must remember that a smart contract automatically executes penalties and consequences of noncompliance, even if they are against the law.

- **It is well implemented**: Although it may seem like a truism, smart contracts implement the clauses they contain—in the form of an algorithm, as we have seen—in software and we know software applications can fail. Therefore, it is not only essential to use a blockchain network for trust but also that implementation is correct. Although the practice of smart contracts is not currently widespread, in the coming years we will see the appearance of more and more smart contract providers that, for free or for a small fee, will offer the coding of rules or clauses in specific blockchain networks. It will be important to trust recognized providers only and, most likely, avoid possible scams and providers with limitations. However, since the smart contract will reside in the corresponding network (Ethereum, for instance) and not in any entity, once you guarantee that the contract is correctly coded and registered, it is irrelevant that the coding provider used disappears later. This is totally different from the contracts that use *escrow* techniques, where there is a third party that oversees verifying that the clauses are fulfilled to release goods or funds from one party to the other. Using escrow would entail a serious problem if the trusted third party disappears as an entity or does not turn out to be as trustworthy. On the contrary, in a smart contract, no third party is needed: even if life were suddenly extinguished on planet Earth, the conditions of the contract would be executed normally, as long as there is only one computer connected to the network (Ethereum, for example) anywhere in the world.

As we have seen, smart contracts are one of the most interesting features of Web 3.0, or the Metaverse. They can be used for many purposes, including releasing funds to the appropriate parties, registering virtual private property, e-commerce, sending formal notifications, or issuing tickets. They will likely start to mature in the physical reality but, for sure, will help develop a lot of new digital services in the Metaverse.

## What Are Nonfungible Tokens (NFTs)

NFT stands for "Nonfungible Token." In plain language, it could be described as a "uniqueness indicator." The reason is that an NFT is simply a piece of code (software) that makes use of Blockchain technology, to serve as a "digital envelop" of a digital asset (an embedded file, irrevocably pasted to this piece of code) that declares its uniqueness. A graphical scheme is provided in Figure 9.3.

If this explanation is a bit difficult to understand, let's see an example: Suppose you take a picture with your smartphone. That photo is naturally stored in a digital file (a digital asset) on the phone. You can share that photo with your friends and family, on your social profile or even make a backup copy in the cloud or on your computer. There is no NFT in there; by their very nature, digital files can be copied indefinitely and will always be the same.

Now, you decide to install an app to convert files to NFT in your phone. Then, when you take the photo, the app processes it and adds a piece of code (a token) based on Blockchain that comes to "stamp" that photo, leaving proof that it is the original. As normally in this technology,

*Figure 9.3 Graphical representation of the information in an NFT token stored in a blockchain*

that token is shared in the corresponding Blockchain network and is stored in its blockchain. You have just turned a photograph into a unique asset, which can be tracked, bought, sold, and stored, even copied, but not duplicated.

Wait a minute … Is not copying the same as duplicating? In the digital world, no. Book readers, and especially authors, can very well understand this difference with the example of printed books; while a publisher can print thousands of copies of a book (copy), when the author signs a book to somebody, it is no longer possible to exactly replicate that book (duplicate). Something similar happens with NFTs in the digital world. The key about NFTs is that they are *encrypted* in the blockchain and only the owner has the *key* to unencrypt the asset in the NFT. But what use can this invention have? Let's first look at the fundamental characteristics of NFTs:

- **Uniqueness**: Each NFT is unique. It is not possible to have two identical NFTs. Each one will have a specific record within the Blockchain network that was used to generate and register it.
- **Indivisibility**: An NFT, once generated, is indivisible. If we create an NFT with a book, for example, any extraction of a

chapter or any deletion (of the copyright page, for example) will be detectable, since it will not match the existing record in the corresponding Blockchain network.

- **Transferability**: When registering an NFT in a Blockchain network, data associated with the digital asset is also registered (usually who owns it, as is the case with cryptocurrencies). Although, as owners, we can make as many backup copies of an NFT as we wish, formally all of them will be associated with our identifier, and, legally, the ownership of the asset will be ours. As the asset will be encrypted, only our personal code will be able to decrypt it, just as it happens with cryptocurrencies (nobody else can access them unless we transfer to their account, being the transaction registered in the Blockchain and, consequently, the *access key* changed to that of the new owner).

- **Scarcity**: Because of all the above, NFTs are scarce by nature. Actually, they are generated one by one, or we could ask an algorithm to generate a finite number of NFTs from a file (a photo, a video, a book, a song, the list of the secret codes to launch the U.S. nuclear arsenal, etc.). This algorithm would do the work of generating them one by one and registering them sequentially in the corresponding Blockchain network on our behalf.

Perhaps now the reason for NFTs is understood a little better; to produce scarce goods in the digital world where, traditionally, everything could be copied ad infinitum. But the possibilities are much more. For instance, one can create a Blockchain network for artists, that allows NFT creators to get royalties each time the NFT is sold—not only when they sell it the first time but also every time this NFT is traded afterward, in the secondary market. This practice is probably impossible or impractical to implement without NFTs, but very easy by using them.

We see that artists need NFTs for sure, but there is even a bigger picture. NFTs will be the future of digital ownership. In the Metaverse, where everything is digitized, we need ownership protection systems like NFTs more than ever. In the short term, NFTs are expected to expand into fields including music, sports, and gaming, as well as other industries in the long term.

## What *Is* Not an NFT?

We constantly hear the NFT acronym in the news. However, not everything tagged as an NFT nowadays is truly an NFT. NFTs are virtual by nature. Knowing that we know about smart contracts as well, we can say an NFT is a smart contract where the asset is a digital item (a file). Thus, your physical home could never be an NFT, a shirt—a physical one—could not be ever an NFT, a car, a watch, Leonardo's Mona Lisa painting … None of them!

A digital photograph of the Mona Lisa made by a famous photographer could be an NFT, a virtual Rolex watch (when they are ready to buy) will be an NFT, and the recording of a song can be an NFT, for instance. There are some items more difficult to assess. For example, the deeds of your home could be an NFT if they were signed under the form of a smart contract and this form was accepted by the national jurisdiction and administration of the country where the property is located. Anyway, your home would never be an NFT, only the deeds. This means that somebody could destroy your physical home even when you keep the NFT of your deeds. Or somebody could occupy your home. Everything would remain the same than using regular deeds because your home will not be an NFT.

Finally, we find many situations where people call a smart contract an NFT. The reason is that NFT is a subset of smart contracts, where the asset is virtual. If the asset is physical, it is a smart contract but not an NFT.

## Summary

In this chapter, we have read about two vital technologies that will make the Metaverse work: smart contracts and NFTs. We got the following ideas:

- A smart contract is a contract associated with a small piece of software based on Blockchain that records the contract terms without a doubt, verifies in real time the fulfillment or not of the different clauses, and launches the appropriate actions, accordingly.

- Smart contracts are seen as *automated* contracts that do not need any third party to attest to the agreement nor execute the clauses. The contract is distributedly recorded in a blockchain.
- For real-time monitoring and execution of the clauses, digital information about the associated events is needed. If the clauses are referred to natural or physical events, IoT sensors or solutions are needed to translate physical to digital information.
- Smart contracts provide security, precision, quick execution, cost-effectiveness, total trust, interruption-free, and autonomy.
- Nonfungible tokens (NFTs) are a particular type of smart contracts where a digital asset or file (a picture, a video, a text, a database) is *encapsulated* as a block of a blockchain and then some conditions are set, like authorship, ownership, value, and so on.
- By nature, NFTs are unique, indivisible, and transferable (they are blocks in a blockchain, so they inherit its features). This makes them scarce and transactable. Given the full traceability provided by Blockchain technology, NFTs can be marketed in much many forms than physical items (e.g., an author could set royalty rules for a digital book or a photo in the second-hand market).
- NFT concept is a bit complex term to understand, and it is frequently misused—unintentionally or on purpose—in the news.

# CHAPTER 10

# How Will I End Up in the Metaverse?

In this chapter, we will see how the Metaverse will come to our lives from different perspectives. As an inevitable trend, the question is not whether you will get impacted by the Metaverse in a positive or negative sense, but *when* and *how*. As shown in Figure 10.1, the enabling technologies are progressively advancing to the right of the typical Gartner's hype curve, fostering the maturity of the Metaverse as well. Let's see the different drivers that will bring the Metaverse over all societies.

## The Metaverse Economic System

The Metaverse economic system runs parallel with the real economic system, and these two systems can be regarded as a parallel economic system (Wen et al. 2013). Once the Metaverse is mature, optimal economic operations of the real economic system will be achieved only through simultaneous management of the parallel economic system. In plain text, *nobody* will escape the Metaverse. First, the Metaverse economic system will be able to provide a detailed description of the knowledge needed in the real economic system, as well as economic theories, procedures, processes, and related operations. As such, it will be used by managers of companies and cities for the purpose of learning and training. Second, since numerous and repeated computational experiments can be easily conducted in the Metaverse, any real economic decisions or proposals impacting real organizations will be evaluated—simulated—and tested in the Metaverse economic system before implementation. Moreover, the results of the computational experiments can also provide predictions for the future economic states of such organizations, as far as the digital model is translated with enough detail to the Metaverse. Third, driven by

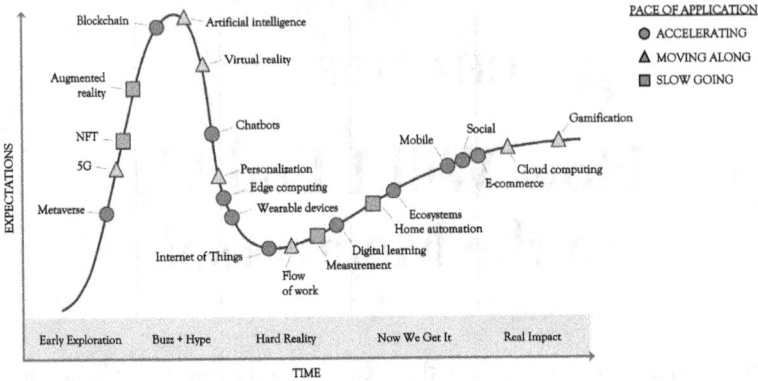

*Figure 10.1 The hype cycle for the Metaverse and other enabling technologies (own elaboration)*

real entities—users and organizations—the Metaverse economic system will emulate the real economic system and provide prescriptions for the real economic system. In a conclusion, we can predict that the Metaverse will be smoothly entering our lives twofold: through tangible isolated applications, mostly related to gaming and socialization, and through the progressive *correlation* between the Metaverse economic system and organizations, as a result of more business processes and managerial decisions being translated to virtual spaces.

Besides, to improve the functionality, accessibility, and governance models of cross-platform 3D multiuser social environments, the backbone of the Metaverse, it will be critical to facilitate a plethora of continuous professional development opportunities in all levels of education (Mystakidis et al. 2021a) so that learning in the Metaverse leads to deep and meaningful learning (Mystakidis et al. 2021b). According to Gartner (Figure 10.2), we are just experiencing the first emerging Metaverse and the roadmap until we enjoy a mature Metaverse that can last nearly 10 years.

## Smart Everything

We are getting accustomed to the prefix "smart" being applied to many technological and nontechnological things. Usually, we refer to a smart "something" when some advanced digital logic with computing capabilities is inserted in that item. For instance, a smartwatch or a smart TV can

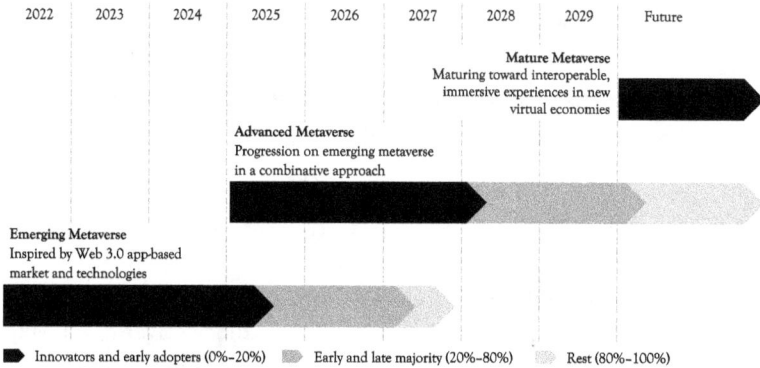

| 2022 | 2023 | 2024 | 2025 | 2026 | 2027 | 2028 | 2029 | Future |

**Mature Metaverse**
Maturing toward interoperable,
immersive experiences in new
virtual economies

**Advanced Metaverse**
Progression on emerging metaverse
in a combinative approach

**Emerging Metaverse**
Inspired by Web 3.0 app-based
market and technologies

► Innovators and early adopters (0%–20%)   Early and late majority (20%–80%)   Rest (80%–100%)

*Figure 10.2 Gartner's evolution spectrum for the Metaverse*

show apps and be connected to the Internet; a smart meter can autonomously read the gas or electricity consumption at home and send it to the utility supplier using wireless Internet, and so on. The Metaverse will leverage smart things to become the predominant scenario for human interaction in record time.

For example, smart contracts seen in Chapter 9 are based on blockchain and have the characteristics of automatic execution and nontampering and can provide an intelligent and efficient solution for management in the Metaverse. Using smart contracts, management systems, modes, rules, and incentive mechanism designs are stored on a blockchain. When the execution conditions of these smart contracts are met, they will automatically execute without manual intervention, which greatly improves the promptness of actions, automation, and the intelligence level of management itself. The use of smart contracts, therefore, will provide decision-making mechanisms for the real world through virtual–real interaction using closed-loop feedback. That way, information will flow between the Metaverse and the physical reality to expand the use of smart contracts to many things that are limited today because they do not provide digitized information that can be managed in a virtual space.

In this point, another *smart* object is essential: smart sensors. Smart sensors are regular sensors (for noise, light, speed, pressure, etc.) equipped with autonomous electronic circuitry that allows them to feed their measures directly into databases or applications, to make them available instantly and seamlessly. Smart sensors are being massively deployed today, and they will have a profound impact on the adoption of the Metaverse. As more physical measures are digitized and uploaded to the digital world, more Metaverse applications will be possible, including more smart contracts whose conditions are based on these digitized measures.

# Social VR

Social VR is the name for the future evolution of social media. It is expected that social media will evolve to work in the Metaverse, allowing users to interact with each other as avatars in the virtual world, communicating and collaborating as if they were in the physical world. The largest company owning social media, Meta (the owner of Facebook, Instagram, and WhatsApp), has already created its own metaverse to start experimenting and deploying new features there, although none of its commercially available social media are still operating there. Even when this could take some time, there are some social VR platforms already available. The most popular are as follows:

- **VRChat** (hello.vrchat.com): The platform allows users to interact with others with user-created 3D avatars and virtual worlds. VRChat is designed primarily for use with VR headsets, but is also usable without VR in a "desktop" mode designed for either a mouse and keyboard or a gamepad. The platform can be used for socializing, developing some games, and even music or dance performances.
- **AltspaceVR** (altvr.com): AltspaceVR is a social VR platform first launched in 2015. In 2017 it was acquired by Microsoft. Some elements of the platform appear in Microsoft Mesh, the experimental VR collaboration suite that is being developed by Microsoft for the business environment. AltspaceVR largely consists of user-generated virtual worlds, which can be visited by other users. This platform is specialized in hosting live virtual events, being regularly home to a wide variety of events from VR church and LGBTQI+ meetups to large business conferences and magic shows. In addition to these

events, AltspaceVR is a social VR platform where individuals can gather, talk, collaborate, and be present in small-to-large virtual groups.

- **Mozilla Hubs** (hubs.mozilla.com): The famous web browser Mozilla has also "created" an open-source social VR platform, called Mozilla Hubs. Hubs is a VR chatroom designed for every VR headset and browser, and an open-source project that explores how communication in MR can come to life. Because it uses web standards (WebVR and eventually WebXR) to deliver the 3D created content, it can support every single MR headset, which is considered a plus for early adoption.

- **Cluster** (cluster.mu): Mostly used in Japan, and following manga comic esthetics, Cluster is a social platform based around bringing together players in virtual spaces, called "virtual worlds." These spaces can be created by Cluster or by fellow players and are free and open to be explored. From beautiful, aesthetic worlds to activity-filled gaming worlds, there are plenty of options to choose from.

- **Bigscreen** (www.bigscreenvr.com): BigScreen allows users to host VR parties with friends. It comes with the ability to display content anywhere users see fit. The main idea behind this platform is to let users livestream their displays to friends in a virtual environment. With BigScreen, users can play their favorite games on a massive screen inside a VR environment or watch any content that would normally be displayed on a regular desktop screen, such as Twitch, Netflix, YouTube, and other videos. One of the benefits is that users can decide on the size of the virtual screen, from 30 inches to an IMAX-size screen. Additionally, the virtual environment where users meet can be anything from a luxury apartment to outer space. The platform features a low-latency positional audio chat functionality, for a more immersive experience. BigScreen represents an important step toward turning VR into an integral part of our daily life.

## Metaverse Apps

More and more, developers will create their catalogs of apps working in the Metaverse. In the meanwhile, we already have a large set of apps using VR or AR. A good list can be found in the open wiki XinReality (xinreality.com). However, we must be careful with many apps that are adding the term "metaverse" as a marketing claim, but which do not have anything to do with Metaverse applications. After Facebook was rebranded as "Meta" in October 2021, the number of apps referring to Metaverse grew up to 552 in less than a quarter, according to Sensor Tower.

It is true that many Metaverse apps will be about gaming, as mentioned in Chapter 2. However, there are other categories expected, as we saw in Chapter 12. Depending on what you do in your daily life, it will be more likely that you enter the Metaverse by using a collaboration tool or an entertainment app, for example. The truth is that, as 3D technology and computing power (CPU/GPU) evolve, a larger share of the current app catalog found for smartphones or desktop computers will create their future versions for the Metaverse. In fact, there are already two major stores for VR applications (Oculus, by Meta, and Viveport, by HTC). Although they are app stores exclusively linked to the devices provided by their respective manufacturers, it is possibly the first step toward true Metaverse repositories.

A parallel path can be envisaged from current mobile apps, mostly found in the Apple Store and Google Play. Much likely, as soon as more VR and wearable devices can connect to smartphones and interact with mobile apps, changes can be expected in the way these stores work today. Many applications about creativity, sports, health care, education, and so on will need to be categorized, somehow, as immersive Metaverse applications. However, convergence between access devices such as VR headsets and smartphones or computers, will be too far in time to think that the near future will be more app stores and more technological segmentation.

## The Natural Path to Adopting the Metaverse

We have just seen that the Metaverse is not expected to smoothly evolve from a point A to a point B. Instead, there are many "points A"

(VR headsets, smartphones, computers …) and much more "points B" (existing and new app stores, web apps …). Consequently, the *natural* path toward the Metaverse adoption will surely consist of a strong fight between large players (e.g., Meta, Microsoft, and Apple) and new entrants. Most of the current applications and technologies we find today as promising seeds for the Metaverse will no longer exist in less than a decade. Some others will converge and become compatible. Some other technologies and standards that will form the true Metaverse do not even exist today.

However, there is a piece of very good news about the Metaverse. It is that the goal for its development is clear: the Metaverse will succeed the *plain* Internet we use today. Of course, the Internet will continue to exist, like how paper exists even when having digital video, but Metaverse will become mainstream for many daily activities and business applications. The threshold is probably related to the massive adoption of VR inexpensive, lightweight glasses, and then, the market opportunity, opened by millions of potential users, will bring more and more applications.

## Summary

In this chapter, we have read about the following ideas:

- The enabling technologies of the Metaverse (AI, VR, IoT …) are quickly evolving and becoming more widely adopted. This will make the Metaverse mature in combination with them, probably faster or slower, depending on the potential applications of each technology of the Metaverse.
- The Metaverse economic system will run in parallel with the current economic system with several connection points. Initially, these points will be very few but, in time, the interconnection will be much stronger.
- Social VR is the evolution of social media, adopting immersive virtual worlds and new features and services.

- This increased connection between users and machines (more and deeper sensing impacts on the body) will boost the use of the Metaverse. Besides gaming, which has been the ignition for the Metaverse's existence, social VR will be of the essence for the maturity of the Metaverse.
- There will be a natural path from current *plain* Internet websites and mobile apps to spatial and immersive ones in the Metaverse. Both worlds will coexist, but most of the activities we perform today using the Internet will be done in the Metaverse in some years.

# CHAPTER 11

# Possibilities in the Metaverse for the Different Industries

The first Metaverse applications have been twofold. From academia, most papers published related to the Metaverse have addressed **education** topics (e.g., an experience using metaverses for teaching mechanical physics to engineering students [Díaz et al. 2020], studying the perception of high school students about using Metaverse in AR learning 2020 experiences in mathematics [Park et al. 2021]). However, in the commercial industry, most developments have addressed games, socialization, and, to an extent, art. But the Metaverse opens immense possibilities for other sectors such as culture, retail, home automation, and even sports, psychology, journalism, politics, and religion, to mention some.

The underlying immersive technologies of the Metaverse will provide different options regarding each potential application, as follows:

- Spatial computing allows the control of computing equipment with natural gestures and speech.
- Brain–computer interfaces enable communication with computing devices exclusively through brain activity for the control of a synthetic limb or to empower paralyzed persons to operate computers.
- The integration of blockchain-based cryptocurrencies (e.g., Bitcoin) and NFTs allow the deployment of innovative virtual economy transactions and architectures.
- On a broader scale, Metaverse-related technologies are expected to cross-pollinate, expand, and be further amplified by exponential technologies such as wireless broadband networks, cloud computing, robotics, AI, and 3D printing.

A good description of the structure of the Metaverse is given by Jon Radoff in the form of seven layers (Figure 11.1). The reason why we present this model here instead of showing it in Chapter 5, where we spoke about how the Metaverse is built, is because the seven layers are very useful to explain the potential applications for the different players around the Metaverse in this chapter.

Contrary to classical approaches like Open Systems Interconnection (OSI) standard or the Transmission Control Protocol/Internet Protocol (TCP/IP) stack used to define the Internet, Radoff's layers go from the highest level to the lowest one. Therefore, the first layer is about the user experience and user-generated content. The second one, called "discovery," is about how the user establishes social interaction and how vendors provide new experiences. Layer 3 is called "creator economy" and refers to the fact that thanks to Blockchain technology and other enabling tools, users will be able to monetize and control content in the Metaverse, keeping traceability and royalties under control. This is the first layer that is closely related to specific technologies. The next one, called "spatial computing" is where all VR engines and solutions to develop 3D immersive worlds and applications work, while the fifth layer is all about "decentralization," that is, enabling algorithms and protocols that support the

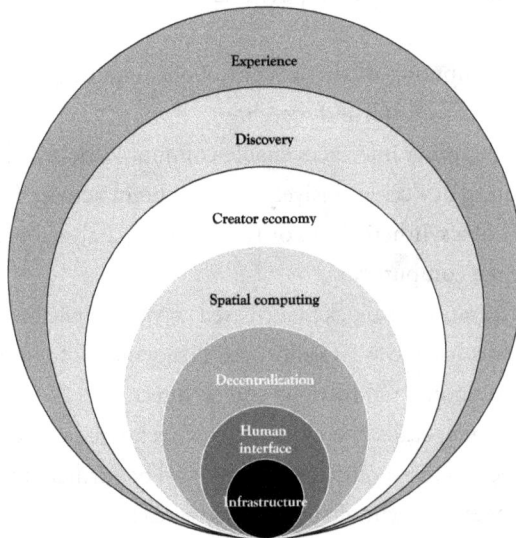

*Figure 11.1 The seven layers of the Metaverse, according to Jon Radoff*

overall physical structure to make the Metaverse work. Layer 6, called "human interface" is about VR headsets, wearable devices, and so on, and finally, the last layer is about the "infrastructure" (hardware) that supports everything.

## Two Popular Examples

If we look for specific applications, the car manufacturer BMW has used the Nvidia **Omniverse** platform to build a fully functional digital twin of one of its automobile factories to reduce operational costs and increase reliability. Many people know that the high level of customization offered by car manufacturers is only possible by following the "just-in-time" methodology: you *configure* your desired car and then that configuration is used to build a car from scratch in a highly robotized process. The problem with this approach is that, when combined with the critical quality aspects associated with vehicles, the *lead* time (the time between the order is sent to the manufacturing plant and the vehicle is ready to be delivered) can be long (months). This forces continuous production (24/7) with very little room for defective parts if you want a profitable business. Both aspects are contradictory: machines normally require to be readjusted and fine-tuned regularly to keep defect ratios low, while engineers need to stop the production line to make such adjustments. With a digital twin, the actual factory can continue 24/7 operation without disruption, while engineers are not in a rush to simulate and improve configurations reliably.

Regarding the Nvidia Omniverse platform, it is worth mentioning that this metaverse uses a standard open language provided by the famous animation movie maker Pixar, called Universal Scene Description (USD). Considering that both companies—Nvidia and Pixar—are market leaders in their fields, the promotion of an open standard is very good news for the deployment of the Metaverse.

Another example of current applications already working as a metaverse (we do not yet have *the Metaverse* as a unified network) is **HoloVerse**, a project undertaken by several telecom companies—Deutsche Telekom, Telefónica, TIM, MobiledgeX, and DoubleMe—to test the best 5G edge cloud network infrastructure for efficient deployment of services in the Metaverse. HoloVerse uses DoubleMe's metaverse solution called "TwinWorld" and the cloud platform of MobiledgeX, to let the three large carriers (DT, Telefónica, and TIM) simulate and test the performance of future Metaverse applications on their networks.

Next, let's review some interesting business opportunities in different application fields.

## Simulation

First, let's clarify what simulation is and what is not. According to the American English Dictionary, a simulation is "a model of a real activity, created for training purposes or to solve a problem." *Simulation* is different from *emulation*, which is "the process of copying something achieved by someone else and trying to do it as well as they have." In Metaverse simulation, the focus is on the purpose of creating a digital model to train or solve a problem, while mere emulation is just creating the model with very good fidelity.

Simulations depicting real-world tasks for educational purposes or to solve certain problems are a universal application in the Metaverse, given its tremendous capability to replicate physical reality. Indeed, we already have very good examples of simulations in the Metaverse, like Microsoft Flight Simulator, which is used not only for gaming but also for professional pilot training purposes.

The aforementioned example of BMW using the Nvidia Omniverse platform for simulating its manufacturing plants is another famous example in this category. In fact, simulation in the Metaverse heavily relies on the concept of "*digital twin*," which will be covered in Chapter 16, as one of the technologies to watch during the next years, related to the Metaverse.

## Gaming

Video games are the most common application for the popularization of the Metaverse. Owing to the immersive experience provided, which can lead to potential addiction as we will see in Chapter 15, the gaming industry embraced the Metaverse, as seen in Chapter 2, since the beginning. In addition to simply use video games for mere entertainment, there is a recent trend to approach difficult tasks of any kind through games to simplify them or encourage the accountable people to do them with less fatigue or more productivity. This technique of using games for other purposes than just entertainment is called *gamification*.

Gamification is extensively used nowadays in marketing campaigns because it has been proven a very good way to better attract the target audience than using other methods such as advertising. Either for marketing purposes or for work-related tasks, the Metaverse opens a tremendous door for gamification. Since payments and personal information will be widely used in the Metaverse, many new applications for gamification will emerge. Additionally, the Metaverse is expected to become one of our main daily "activities" regarding time dedication. Therefore, marketing agencies, employers, media broadcasters, and other organizations will surely put an eye on this new channel of communication—and persuasion.

But gaming will have many more potential applications than those we can currently imagine. For example, there is a proposal to use a VR system for neurorehabilitation exercises called INREX-VR (Stanica et al. 2020). It captures real-time user movements in a gamified environment and executes complex movements to encourage self-improvement and competition to improve the patient's quality of life.

## Workplace

Another natural evolution from current applications to the Metaverse is found in the workplace, more specifically in virtual meetings or video-conferences. The push given to remote working in recent years has spread in many homes and offices, a bunch of videoconference solutions, like Zoom, Microsoft Teams, Google Meet, GoToMeeting, Skype, and many more. However, these tools provide just a flat view of all participants on the screen and plain sound. They are far from being immersive, which not only has demonstrated to provoke fatigue but also limits the number of potential applications and tasks to be performed remotely by employees. The Metaverse could radically transform the experience of meeting people in business environments. To solve the lack of spatial sense in online

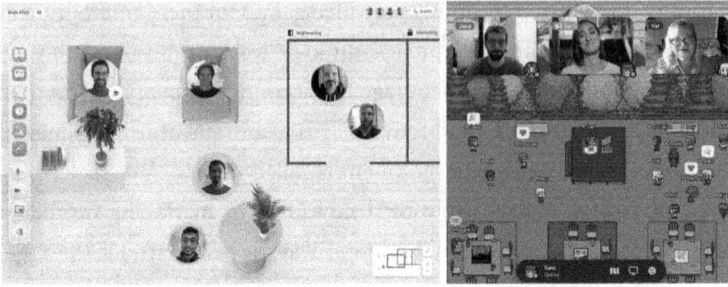

*Figure 11.2 Screenshots of TeamflowHQ (left) and GatherTown (right)*

conferences, the Metaverse can provide not only 3D meetings in much more realistic *virtual rooms* but also spatial audio, so one can focus ears on the direction of the person who is speaking and the noise coming from other participants will not be so disturbing as in plain conferences today.

An attempt to replicate physical interaction in the office is currently made by some companies that provide a 2D representation of a virtual office where employees can interact. Some examples are Teamflow (www .teamflowhq.com) and Gather (www.gather.town), depicted in Figure 11.2, which also use spatial audio technology to provide speech and footstep sounds according to distance, to make the interactive experience more realistic. However, these tools are far from being extensively adopted because of their limited applicability to solving business tasks. There is still a lot to do in the Metaverse to deliver real valuable applications for the workplace.

## Socialization

As an evolution of Second Life, the primitive game where socialization was crucial to succeed, the Metaverse is expected to boost the relevance of digital technologies in social interaction. When people interact in the Metaverse instead of the physical reality, not only are geographic barriers broken—like what happens today with social media—but also the level of interaction can be adjusted at the user's will. On one end, a user can keep privacy at the desired point, for example, by not revealing his or her real name, phone, or address. On the other, he or she can favor a more distended environment, giving rise to fantasies that were unacceptable in the physical world. To an extent, this happens today with social media, but the Metaverse will provide such a level of immersion and attractiveness to our senses that some people will even feel their lives in the Metaverse are more real than their physical ones.

In addition to this, there are some social changes expected because of the Metaverse. For instance, because avatars change skin color and gender as desired, they have the advantage of reducing preconceived notions about social discrimination in conversations. This has been already proven by some authors recently.

## Culture

Another important outcome the Metaverse can provide is related to cultural life (e.g., museums and performances). The Metaverse can better realize digital tourism and digital exhibition. The development of digital twin technology (explained later in Chapter 16) and interactive technology allows users to break through the limitations of time, space, and other factors, freely visit scenic spots around the world and get an immersive experience. The number of immersive applications in this topic is gradually increasing. It is now possible to visit some of the most important museums virtually (e.g., La Louvre in Paris) or attend some concerts and events from home. However, although the limited capacity and time constraints of a concert hall are solved when making it available in the Metaverse, there is still a lack of textures and fine details that make the experience poorer than attending physically. This will surely evolve as more solutions are developed and more users demand such events and experiences.

Lastly, as a new social form of society, the Metaverse will give rise to new cultural forms and methods of cultural creation. The development of interactive technology and the further improvement of immersion can effectively promote the development of virtual idols and pure virtual concerts. It could happen that some of these idols (singers, dancers, artists ...) are not famous only in the virtual space—the Metaverse—but they only exist there (be a creation of AI and do not have a counterpart in the physical world).

## Event Planning

Virtual reality will revolutionize the way events are organized. Events can be anything from concerts to seminars. The advantage for event planning proliferation in the Metaverse is that they can use a VR builder that is already available for socialization, or even gaming, to arrange private parties, seminars, or concerts. Even AR, where users still physically meet but augmented information appears on certain objects, circumstances, or interactions, could be the near future of event planning in the Metaverse.

## Marketing

It is obvious that marketing exists wherever business is. In the Metaverse, we can find two marketing approaches, one related to companies using Metaverse experiences to make people buy their physical products and another consisting of pure Metaverse marketing, where brands use marketing techniques in the Metaverse to make people buy or use their products in the Metaverse.

Economic activity is important in the Metaverse, as it contributes to creating an ecosystem around it. We are not going to dive into all opportunities the Metaverse provides for marketing. It could take tens of pages to describe all those. Just think about the transformation suffered by marketing because of social media adoption. Then extrapolate that to the immersive experience offered by the Metaverse. There are many companies providing guidance to other businesses to succeed in their marketing strategy in the Metaverse, like McKinsey, the Global Institute of Advisors (www.gia.institute), and Influencer Marketing Hub, among others.

## Education

When speaking of education, audiovisual-based education is an important application of the Metaverse, with a high potential for popularization. Experiential education is important because what you see in writing and how you feel while experiencing it are different. For example, radiation is difficult to experience, so you may preconceive that it is simply dangerous. It is possible to measure the positive educational effects when analyzing and experiencing radioactivity technically and scientifically in the Metaverse. It is demonstrated that the Metaverse provides a better learning attitude, more enjoyment, and better performance compared to just using standard video presentations and textbooks.

Additionally, the Metaverse will help in the development of remote or virtual laboratories. There are some initiatives, mostly sponsored by universities and research centers, to build remote laboratories that could be exploited not only by university students more efficiently but also by students from other universities as well. The use of remote laboratories (highly robotized so a student can use equipment and parts remotely and watch everything through a digital interface, frequently equipped with a camera to see the experiment in real time) could become a much more immersive experience when using the Metaverse. However, the highest potential relies on the fact that fully virtual laboratories could be developed in the Metaverse, dramatically reducing the cost, allowing many more students to have access to experimentation that otherwise would be impossible to afford, and reducing the potential harm risk of certain laboratory experiments.

However, using the Metaverse for educational purposes still requires a lot of effort. First, it is not yet clear about the advantages and disadvantages of such a multiuser virtual environment for education, but furthermore, the Metaverse requires accessing devices and content, as seen before, which is not yet available for most of the educational topics. Finally, teachers will need to learn about educating using the Metaverse, in the short term, and probably *inside* the Metaverse, in the future. Although some experiences have been addressed on using the Metaverse for education, like the one to use Metaverse in problem-based learning (PBL), and another for safety training for children in the outdoor environment with the VR Kinect sensor and the Unity game engine, everything is still in the experimental phase and the market opportunity for education is just emerging.

## Other Opportunities

We have seen some of the most impactful opportunities related to the Metaverse. However, as a transforming industry, the Metaverse will impact many other sectors and activities. For instance, as a virtual world parallel to reality, the Metaverse will use digital twin technology to further develop smart cities. Digital twin technology can digitally map the physical world, fully capture urban data such as people, vehicles, objects, and space, and form a visible, controllable, and manageable digital twin city. It can improve the efficiency of resource utilization, optimize urban management and services, and improve the quality of life of the citizens.

As another example, in the psychology field, the Metaverse can help with psychotherapy. It will be able to provide help in constructing virtual relaxing environments and communicating and interacting with virtual characters as well.

The world is starting to welcome the Metaverse in many forms. It is a matter of time and imagination that new applications and services will emerge, everywhere.

## Summary

In this chapter, we have read about the following ideas around possible opportunities that the Metaverse will bring:

- The seven layers of the Metaverse, proposed by Jon Radoff, explain how the Metaverse will be built, from the required hardware to the highest experiential layer.
- The Metaverse can be useful for simulation, given that it can reproduce the physical reality with high fidelity.
- We have seen how gaming is fostering the development of new VR and human–machine interaction technologies.
- Regarding the workplace, some initiatives that emulate the physical office in the Metaverse have been commented on, using spatial audio and dynamic movement of avatars in a virtual office.
- We have shown the possible benefits of the Metaverse for socialization, especially fighting social discrimination and controlling privacy.
- In the cultural space and tourism, the Metaverse may completely transform the experience of traveling and visiting

touristic attractions or remote places (physically, virtually, or using a hybrid combination). Additionally, new forms of art and culture will emerge from the Metaverse itself.

- Events (corporate events, concerts, seminars …) will also transform, mostly through incorporating VR and AR.
- Completely new marketing expertise for the Metaverse will be needed, as even though some current methods and techniques will remain valid, many others will need to be profoundly revisited.

# CHAPTER 12

# What Is There Inside the Metaverse

The Metaverse is an emerging ecosystem that will be dramatically expanded in the coming years. However, we can find some solutions already available. Although most of them are related to video games, we can also find some interesting alternative applications. In this chapter, we have picked just a diversified group to illustrate the current maturity state of the Metaverse.

## Decentraland, a New Socializing Metaverse

Among the earliest attempts to build a metaverse, Decentraland is a gaming or socializing platform where the user experience is comparable to Second Life and Minecraft, already described in Chapter 2. The exciting thing about Decentraland is that it makes use of NFTs and smart contracts. Decentraland is supported by the Ethereum blockchain and makes extensive use of virtual reality (VR). An idea about how Decentraland virtual space looks is shown in Figure 12.1.

## Horizon Home (by Meta)

Horizon Home (Figure 12.2) started with just very few features in the last quarter of 2021: the possibility to invite other avatars to your virtual home for a chat and watch some videos. However, it is an interactive way of socializing with friends online, and more features are expected as software developers add more applications. Meta wants to offer users fully customized virtual environments and incoming features will go in that direction. It is expected that Facebook Messenger will soon be available

*Figure 12.1 An example scene of the Decentraland metaverse*

*Figure 12.2 The current aspect of Meta Horizon Home solution for the Metaverse*

in Horizon Home and, progressively, Meta's social networks (Facebook, Instagram, and WhatsApp) may become integrated in this metaverse.

Horizon Home is not the only project Meta is working on related to the Metaverse. The technological giant acquired Oculus Quest, the largest VR headset manufacturer, to invest in this direction, and changed the name to Meta Quest. Although Horizon Home seems initially targeted at entertainment, Meta wants to also target the workplace. As an example, multitasking in 2D apps is currently supported by the Meta Quest headset, and this feature may expand as time goes on, eventually making its way to 3D apps as well. The company plans to add more apps in the future, including Dropbox and Slack, which are two essential tools for remote employees. The integration of Meta Quest applications with Horizon Home space will be a huge leap toward the generalized adoption of the Metaverse.

## Bloktopia, a Metaverse Inside a Building

Bloktopia is a metaverse with a virtual skyscraper standing 21 stories tall. This number is a tribute to bitcoin, which has a maximum limit of 21 million. Bloktopia users can do pretty much everything a metaverse is expected to offer: they can create and customize avatars, learn cryptocurrency skills, attend social activities, buy and sell part of the virtual building space, advertise their products, and more. The exciting feature of Bloktopia is its builder tool. The residents of this VR skyscraper can create game elements like obstacles and artwork inside the virtual space and earn money by showing it to others.

Unlike many others, Bloktopia uses Polygon's blockchain. Some users prefer this blockchain over more prominent ones like Ethereum, claiming it is faster and cheaper.

## The Sandbox, a Seed for the True Metaverse

The Sandbox metaverse is one of the most compelling metaverse experiences current technology can provide. The virtual environment uses the Ethereum blockchain, which is one of the most reputable and dependable blockchains available at present. Moreover, Ethereum can be used to create digital goods, which is what the Sandbox metaverse is all about.

The decentralization aspect of Sandbox is another interesting feature to observe. Sandbox's decentralized governance, the NFT-based economy, and in-game token showcase how regulations and community management will operate in the metaverse. As far as user interaction is concerned, the Sandbox is very similar to Decentraland. In Sandbox, players can buy digital plots of land and then share their experiences on top of them with other players. The mix of decentralization, social engagement, and gameplay provide the perfect environment for a fun and lucrative metaverse.

## Meta Hero, a Notary in the Metaverse

The logic behind Meta Hero is unique and intriguing. The company has come up with a great vision to exploit the Metaverse. Meta Hero is basically an NFT bank. Suppose you want to lend your NFTs to other metaverses like Sandbox or Decentraland. All you need to do is enter Everdome. Everdome is a virtual place equipped with virtual cameras that capture images of anything that stands inside, whether it is an individual or an object. Your virtual product (a created or scanned 3D object, a painting, etc.) can then be turned into an NFT and be rented out to users in other metaverses under your consideration.

## Enjin, a Tool for Developers of Virtual Items

Enjin software enables developers to create and manage virtual goods linked to the Ethereum blockchain. What is genuine about Enjin is using blockchains to manage in-game items across many different properties. In addition, Enjin intends to reduce the high fees associated with digital transactions in some popular blockchains.

Another aspect of Enjin that sets it apart from others is its work on fraud issues. Enjin has released software development kits that make it possible for users to create digital assets on the Ethereum blockchain and integrate them into games and applications. The idea is to ensure that every asset is customized to fit the desired platform and recorded as a smart contract. In this way, speed, cost, and security are present when using cryptocurrencies.

## Star Atlas, an Immersive Intergalactic Experience

Star Atlas is another game developed as a metaverse that uses the Solana blockchain for item transactions. The game is built with Unreal Engine, which makes it possible to create highly realistic games. The goal of the game is space exploration. You do so by siding with a faction, creating civilizations, and, of course, setting intergalactic economies. The economy is supported by the in-game ATLAS token, as well as by the POLIS token, which is required to manipulate the options in the game related to cryptocurrencies.

Although there is nothing special about the game, it is illustrative because it is probably the best combination of blockchain technology for in-game tokens that control economic parameters, and realistic immersive graphics.

## Summary

This chapter has given an overview of what is there already regarding the Metaverse, summarized as follows:

- Decentraland is an emerging virtual space for gaming or socializing. Some relevant companies are watching how it evolves closely.
- Meta's proposal for the Metaverse, "Horizon Home," was recently launched with very limited applications (mostly experimental) but, given the fact that Meta is the owner of Facebook, Instagram, and WhatsApp, among many other companies, it is a major player to follow.
- Bloktopia is a metaverse in the form of a virtual building. It is a highly interesting experiment about how people react to purchasing virtual property, among other things.
- The Sandbox is similar to Decentraland. It is another interesting solution to watch, especially until we reach a more stable ecosystem of winning technologies.
- Meta Hero is an NFT bank that facilitates transparent NFT transactions. It is another interesting experiment to investigate.
- Enjin is targeted at Metaverse software developers. It is intended to be like the Github for the Metaverse, with expanded features.
- Star Atlas is probably the best combination of Blockchain technology for in-game tokens that control economic parameters and realistic, immersive graphics.

# CHAPTER 13

# Is the Metaverse Secure?

The Metaverse is expected to become a central activity in our daily lives. It is absolutely a priority to be sure that it is secure enough to host critical and private information, as well as most of the central processes and tasks that conform to society. Even though commercial applications that may be considered the beginning of the Metaverse, like social VR platforms, employ secure communication protocols to protect transmitted data, the Metaverse may still lead to many security concerns, such as users' identification information. Since many Metaverse applications will require users to access using VR headsets, they often need to identify themselves with biometric information, which could be a target of security attacks (Mathis et al. 2021). Digital twins in the Metaverse, which will be explained in detail in Chapter 16, also need protection. There will be many complex machine learning (ML) models for supporting digital twins, which in turn influence objects in the physical world. If these models were attacked, there would be unpredictable effects in the physical world. Moreover, wearable devices and sensors that will be used to feed data or interact with Metaverse applications will continuously collect personal information (e.g., biometric information or user behavior), which could rise privacy concerns.

In this chapter, the issues associated with privacy and continuous monitoring are shown, followed by what kind of information devices such as VR headsets and wearables can collect about individuals when using the Metaverse and what kind of attacks and data leaks individuals can suffer in the Metaverse, including deepfake and alternate representations. Another point of concern related to the security and reliability of the Metaverse is related to trust and accountability, which will be analyzed next. Finally, we will show how service designers and software developers can follow some ethical approaches in the Metaverse to solve the identified privacy issues.

## Privacy in the Metaverse

Digital traces of users can be tracked in the Metaverse to obtain the users' real-world identity, and other sensitive data, such as location, shopping preferences, and even financial records. Guaranteeing privacy is essential in shaping the social Metaverse. According to our current experience with social networks, applying privacy-preserving schemes is not an easy task, given the huge amount of data stored and interactions that take place every minute. When we add a spatial web that considerably multiplies the possibilities to share data and the types of data shared, the complexity to preserve privacy is also multiplied. If, as an example, a user navigates a shopping mall in the Metaverse, and another user follows and records all the things the user buys and the journey throughout the mall, this information could be used to perform social engineering and be used with malevolent purposes. We can say that a user's followers in social networks barely see what the user does, while a "follower" in the Metaverse could collect almost the same information, or even more, than a "true follower" in the physical world. There is still a long way until it is possible to *turn off* a person from following an avatar in the Metaverse as we can do in current social media.

Another question related to privacy is the need for regulation in the Metaverse, that can protect private property, human rights, dignity, and so on, like in the physical world. Also, "virtual police" and an appropriate legal system (laws) will be needed to ensure a peaceful social interaction. Let's assume that it is possible to buy or build virtual homes in the Metaverse, but no rule exists to refrain other users from freely entering someone else's home and seeing or using any of the virtual assets there.

As in all emerging technologies, there is a long path to see privacy maturity in the Metaverse. There are several attempts in the literature to increase users' privacy in the Metaverse, although all of them seem poorly effective or unpractical. A *classical* approach taken from the real world is to disguise users' avatars by periodically changing their appearance. Some more innovative technics are making it invisible for certain periods or sensible actions, or something called "social clone." This involves creating multiple clones of each user in the Metaverse to confuse the attackers that try to stalk individuals. Such a privacy measure may solve the privacy problem, but it creates an even bigger problem by forcing users to have multiple representations in the Metaverse, not to mention millions of clones roaming around the Metaverse, which will confuse more than just the attackers and make service customization, for example, much more difficult.

It is more likely that privacy plans in the Metaverse include a combination of different schemes where the user or the service provider can enable a particular privacy option for each situation. There is an interesting privacy scheme proposed that combines various privacy techniques such as virtual clone, private copy, mannequin, avatar lockout, avatar disguise, teleport, and invisibility, as shown in Table 13.1 (Falchuk et al. 2018). There are also suggestions that make no sense in the field of the Metaverse, like those that argue that the jurisdiction of the user's country should be applied in the Metaverse, especially regarding privacy and social interaction. After realizing how complex are the topics about Internet services for legal jurisdictions today and considering that the Metaverse is a virtual world that does not need to have a match with the physical space, it seems nonsense to think this way. However, it is likely that we will see

**Table 13.1 Privacy-preserving schemes in the Metaverse**

| Privacy scheme | Description |
| --- | --- |
| Avatar cloning | Creation of multiple avatar clones that look identical to confuse privacy intruders. |
| Disguise | The ability of users to switch multiple disguised avatars. |
| Mannequin | Replacing the avatar with a bot that mimics the user's behavior and teleport the user to another location in case of suspected stalking. |
| Invisibility | Allow the avatar to become temporary invisible to prevent it from being tracked by privacy intruders or bots. |
| Teleport | The ability of the avatar to instantly teleport to other location in the Metaverse. |
| Private worlds | Create temporary and private copies of a portion of the Metaverse (e.g., a park) only accessible to one user and merge it accordingly to the main fabric of the Metaverse once the action is finished. |
| Lockout | Some parts of the Metaverse are temporarily locked out for private use for some avatars. |

some attempts from governments in this way, at least at the beginning of the Metaverse.

Anyhow, it is advisable to learn from past experiences in the Internet space and avoid similar problems in the Metaverse in the future. It is better to address potential privacy issues in the earlier stage when the Metaverse ecosystem is still taking shape, rather than waiting for the future, when the problem will be so entrenched in the ecosystem that any solution to address privacy concerns would require a redesign from scratch. We can learn from the example of the third-party cookies-based advertisement technology. The targeted marketing model leverages cookies that keep track of users to provide personalized advertisements, but it does not consider privacy aspects. After General Data Protection Regulation (GDPR) in Europe enforced privacy on any digital service, the result has been a tremendous effort to make the cookie system survive and an annoying user experience each time a webpage is visited.

The problem with privacy is that it slows down the development of digital services and customization. Most of the digital services today are based on the analysis of big data coming from users and the use of AI to extract valuable insight about trends, facts, and user behavior. When privacy regulation becomes more restrictive, users' personal data are kept safer at the expense of poorer service experience. In fact, users typically show a dual posture regarding privacy: on the one hand, people seem to not pay attention to any requirement to access new services without realizing its implications (e.g., a hotel booking app asks access to the microphone and camera of your smartphone and it seems there is no problem in accepting it and installing the app because the value of the service provided seems to be worth it). On the other hand, they show very strong negative reactions when the perceived use of data is not what the user expected, no matter if that was the initial purpose declared in the software license agreement or not (very few people usually read it). Probably, one of the most famous examples is the Facebook and Cambridge Analytica scandal, where the latter company extracted high-level information from the raw data *voluntarily* shared by Facebook users. For any reason, this project became mediatic and triggered a public outcry to the extent that Facebook was summoned by the U.S.

Congress and the UK Parliament to hearings, and Cambridge Analytica went bankrupt soon after.

However, even when restricting data collection in favor of privacy would greatly diminish the potential innovations that the Metaverse ecosystem could enable, the fact is that this task could be very difficult, given the huge amount of data and data types shared in the Metaverse. As in many other topics seen, the Metaverse means an additional increase of the complexity we see nowadays on the Internet.

## Data to Be Protected and Deepfake

Internet-connected devices such as wearables (sensors and small devices that you wear, like a smartwatch, a blood pressure sensor, or a sweating sensor) allow monitoring and collection of users' data. This data can be processed to extract information in multiple ways. Sometimes, the obtained information using advanced analytics algorithms is not even known by the users themselves. Additionally, users may not even know that personal data is being recorded, for instance, the GPS location, the entrance or movement in a shop, or what is spoken at home. Digital devices can collect several types of data: personal information (e.g., physical, cultural, economic), users' behavior (e.g., habits, choices), and communications (e.g., metadata related to personal communications). In the case of VR— the primary device used to *display* the Metaverse—the new approaches to enable more immersive environments (e.g., haptic devices, wearables to track fine-grained users' movements) can threaten users in new ways.

The Metaverse can be seen as a digital copy of the physical reality, for example, buildings, streets, and individuals. Additionally, as we have already seen, it can also build things that do not exist in physical reality, such as a live concert by Frank Sinatra or a Roman circus race. The Metaverse can be perceived as a social *microcosmos* where players (individuals or even artificial players built up on other observed individuals' behavior by applications) can exhibit realistic social behavior. In this ecosystem, the privacy and security perceptions of individuals can follow the real behaviors.

The first category of data that can be found in the Metaverse is related to individuals creating avatars using similar personal information such as gender, age, skin color, name, and other attributes. In addition to the information *declared* by users, for such an immersive experience, the Metaverse takes data directly from the physical world (e.g., users' hand movements, and 3D recordings of places). This directly relates to the use of **biometric data**. For example, some sensors attached to the user's body (e.g., gyroscopes to track the head and hand movements) can control an avatar more realistically. As we will see in the next section, in addition to the usual VR head-mounted displays that we have already seen, wearables such as gloves and special suits can enable new interaction approaches to provide a more realistic and immersive user experience in the Metaverse. These devices can allow users to control their avatar using gestures and render haptic feedback to display more realistic interactions. The goal of capturing such biometric information is to merge the physical reality with the digital world. However, all these biometric data that can render more immersive experiences also open new privacy threats to users. Therefore, there exists a need to protect such information against attacks.

Another sort of data used in the Metaverse that deserves special attention is **digital twins**. Digital twins are virtual objects created to reflect physical ones. These digital objects are not only intended to resemble the physical appearance of their physical counterparts but also to emulate the physical performance or behavior of the related real-world objects. Digital twins will enable *clones* of real-world objects and systems in the Metaverse.

To protect digital twins, the Metaverse must ensure that the digital twins created and implemented are original. In this regard, the Metaverse requires a trust-based information system to protect them. Blockchain is proposed as a potential method by several works. Some authors propose a blockchain-based system to store health data electronically (e.g., biometric data) in records that digital twins can use. As we have already seen in Chapter 9, Blockchain technology can enable new markets based on NFTs. This will allow digital twin owners to sell them as unique assets to other users in the Metaverse.

But, on top of all data types that can be found in the Metaverse, the most challenging is probably **deepfakes**. A deepfake is considered an artificial composition in which a real person is represented so realistically in a dynamic environment (normally a video or a 3D virtual space) that it is nearly impossible to distinguish the recreation of the person from the actual person. The world is a combination of the concepts "deep learning" and "fake" because the use of deep learning technologies is involved to produce the fakes. Considering the importance of avatars and digital spaces in the Metaverse, deepfakes opens a door to severe privacy and trust issues in the Metaverse. Users can have trouble differentiating authentic virtual subjects and objects from deepfakes or alternate representations aiming to scam them. Even in its softer form, scammers can use this technique to create a sense of urgency, fear, or other emotions that lead the users to reveal personal information. For example, a scammer can create an avatar that resembles a friend of the victim to extract some personal information from the latter. A more sophisticated approach is the use of **dark patterns** to influence users into unwanted or unaware decisions. Dark patterns are obtained from clandestine observation of the user's behavior to lead him or her into a specific action. For example, the scammer can know what a user likes to buy in the Metaverse and design a deepfake product that the user will buy without noticing it is not the original one. Some typical dark patterns are shown in Table 13.2.

*Table 13.2 Typical dark patterns used today in some websites and apps*

| Dark pattern | Description |
|---|---|
| Forced continuity | A free trial offers is changed to a paid scheme without warning the user. |
| Deliberate misdirection | The user's attention is lead to the most expensive option, hiding the cheaper (or free) solution. |
| Bait and switch | Use a convention, pattern, or illusion to make the user falsely assume something. |
| Hidden costs | At checkout time, unexpected new costs appear. |
| Roach motel | The start (subscription, sign up) is easy; quitting is very hard. |
| Obscured pricing | The pricing scheme makes it very hard to compare. |
| Disguised ads | Advertising that looks like another type of content is used. |
| Privacy suckering | Force the user to share more private info than required. |
| Growth hacking through spamming | The user is used for promotion or diffusion without his or her knowledge. |
| Sneak into basket | A random additional item appears in the user's basket at the checkout. |
| Roadblock | A pop-up interrupts the user's intended action. |
| Misinformation | Different appealing (color, language, etc.) is used to confuse the user. |

## Trust Inside the Metaverse

Any solution that wants to become widely adopted must be trustable. Trust is related to feelings and, in fact, for the Metaverse to become mainstream, it will only need to be perceived as trustable by users, which mostly depends on the perceived trust and the accountability in the event of unintended consequences. The problem is that even today, the Internet lacks trust. Recirculated news that are not checked against facts, rumors, disinformation … Everything is on the table, as a result of the combination of speed and large coverage provided by social media. The Metaverse will likely be much worse because of the multiplication of channels, the increased level of interaction with users, and the natural growth of the digital universe over time. Thus, one of the foremost challenges of the Metaverse will be to establish a verifiable trust mechanism.

Additionally, trust is a serious matter when speaking of elderly people that do not fully understand or feel comfortable with digital technologies. And the Metaverse has the potential to become the main driver to solve a social problem impacting this group, namely loneliness. Elderly people are more vulnerable to online scams and frauds and, expecting a diverse set of Metaverse services addressed to them, solving trust issues in the Metaverse is a priority for this group.

On the positive side, compared to the regular Internet we know today, the Metaverse has the power to provide *situational awareness*. Situational awareness is the perception of environmental elements and events with respect to time or space, the comprehension of their meaning, and the projection of their future status. It is something that we normally have in the physical world. It is a concept widely used in flight training, where the pilot needs to understand what is happening inside and outside the aircraft as better as possible. The immersive nature of the Metaverse will help provide situational awareness far better than current websites, social media, or apps. Some research on building trust by providing situational awareness has already demonstrated the correlation between both concepts, for example, by adding a situational awareness display in taxis to let passengers know where they are and the points of interest around them, in real time (Chang et al. 2019). The Metaverse could utilize the same approach of proving such information to the user's view in an unobtrusive manner, to provide a full understanding of what is happening around.

Reliability is also considered an important aspect of trust. Users should be able to rely on the Metaverse technologies to handle their data in the way they expect to. Recent advances in trusted computing have paved a path for hardware/crypto-based trusted execution environments (TEE) in mobile devices. A TEE provides for secure and isolated code execution and data processing (cryptographically sealed memory and storage) as well as remote attestation (configuration assertions). Thus, the critical operations on user's data, such as bank transactions or health-related information management, can be done using TEEs. However, this technology is yet to be fully developed for the Metaverse services.

Another aspect of trust, that will also impact the Metaverse, is the problem of users' natural overtrust in certain things. People tend to trust products and services from big brands very easily. Society often relies on reputation as the predominant metric to decide whether to trust a product or service from a given brand. However, in the current data-driven economy, where user information is a commodity, even big brands have been reported to engage in practices aimed to learn about the user as much as possible, sometimes trespassing the limits of privacy and even the regulation of certain countries, that is, Google giving access of users' e-mails to the third parties (Cuthbertson 2018). If we extrapolate this concern to the Metaverse, where human-like interactions take place, the misuse of the related information by third parties can cause significant physiological trauma to users. The IEEE Global Initiative on Ethics of Autonomous and Intelligent Systems recommends that, upon entering any virtual realm, users should be provided a "hotkey" tutorial on how to rapidly exit the virtual experience and information about the nature of algorithmic tracking and mediation within any environment (Morrow et al. 2021).

## Accountability in the Metaverse

Accountability is likely to be one of the major topics of concern in realizing the full potential of the Metaverse. Despite the technological advances making ubiquitous and pervasive computing a reality, many of the potential benefits could be limited if people are comfortable with the experience. Accountability is of the essence for trust, and it is not just related to service providers' accountability but also to users' accountability itself.

Content moderation policies that detail how platforms and services will treat user-generated content are often used in traditional social media to hold users accountable for the content that they generate. Although this can be directly extrapolated to the Metaverse, in this new universe, users are likely to interact with each other through their avatars, which obfuscates the user's identity to a certain extent. Moreover, recent advances in multimodal ML can be used for machine-generated 3D avatars or, something more complex regarding accountability, users' avatars could have some autonomous or semiautonomous behavior, something like what happens in autonomous driving. Suppose you want that your own avatar in the Metaverse be more social and, thus, use a service to move it autonomously when you are offline to interact with other avatars, learning from the expressions you use and the places you visit. Then suppose that your avatar autonomously goes to a place forbidden by your country's law (your physical, real country). It may happen that your avatar does illegal things autonomously and, while you placidly sleep, the police burst into your home and arrest you.

As seen, moderation in the Metaverse will find difficulties in distinguishing in which cases the given avatar embodies human user actions or is governed by a machine. To add more complexity, since humans are entitled to the freedom of expression, some measures to initially protect users by limiting the actions that can be done in the Metaverse by avatars (so everyone can sleep well), could be taken as censorship. Let's remember what happens in real life: they say you cannot kill a person but, in fact, you can. Afterward, you will go to jail or suffer the death penalty, but you can. Would it be right—or even technically possible—to restrict crime or harmful actions in the Metaverse by implementing rules in the Metaverse apps? To make things even more complicated, people's rights and the law is different for each country, so what would be the standard in the Metaverse? A possible solution could be to utilize the constitutional rights extended to users in each location to design the content moderation for that location. But, in the online world, users often cross over the physical boundary, thus this solution may not be feasible.

Another aspect of accountability in the Metaverse comes from how users' data are handled, since devices to access the Metaverse, as we will see in the next section, inherently collect much more sensitive information than the traditional smart devices. Privacy protection regulations like GDPR rely on the user's consent and "right to be forgotten" to address this problem but, frequently, users are not entirely aware of the potential risks and invoke their "right to be forgotten" after some unintended consequences have already happened. To tackle this issue, the Metaverse could follow the principles of **data minimization**, where only the minimum amount of user data necessary for the basic function is collected, and the principle of **zero knowledge**, where the systems retain the user's data only as long as it is needed. Another direction worth exploring is using blockchain technology to operationalize the pipeline for data handling, which always follows the fixed set of policies that have been already consented to. Thus, users can always keep track of their data.

However, there is another option taken from the traditional IT space, which is auditing. It has often been used to ensure that data controllers are accountable to their stakeholders. Auditors are often certified third parties that do not have a conflict of interest with the data controllers. Initially, auditing could be used in the Metaverse as well. However, besides the huge amount of data generated in the Metaverse, auditing faces a challenge regarding how to audit secondary data that were created from the user's data, but not by the user itself. Normally, although there are regulations to ensure a certain level of protection for users' data, there is no explicit clarity about secondary data. This issue also relates the data ownership in the Metaverse, which is still under debate.

Apart from data collection, accountability in the Metaverse goes much beyond since unintended consequences can cause not only psychological damage but also physical harm. For example, the use of augmented reality (AR) to guide drivers or pedestrians may cause life-threatening accidents. Regulatory bodies are still debating how to set up liabilities for incidents triggered by machines that take away users' full attention. We all remember when, in 2018, a self-driving Uber car—which had a human driver—killed a pedestrian in Arizona. The accident could have been avoided if the human operator's full attention were on the road. However, mandating full human attention all the time also diminishes the role of these assistive technologies. Regulatory bodies will need to consider broader contexts in the Metaverse to decide whether the liability in such scenarios belongs to the user, the device manufacturer, or any other third parties.

## Ethical Principles and Designs for the Metaverse

The Metaverse is expected to achieve worldwide proportions, creating several challenges to protect the users in such a broad spectrum. Thus, regulations and laws in this environment should translate into continuous monitoring of users (e.g., chat logs and conversations) to ban those who have been reported by others or break some rules. This approach resembles some governance, which can interfere with the experience in the Metaverse but, without any global control, it could become anarchy and chaos. As in the case of the Internet, countries will regulate some aspects of the Metaverse in their territories but, as we already know, the frontiers in the digital space are not the same as in geography.

Some authors have proposed the gradual implementation of tools to allow groups to control their members and interact with other groups under federation models. This way, users in the Metaverse could create neighborhoods with specific rules, like specific areas where only users with some affinities can enter. Technologies such as blockchain could also allow enforcing users to follow the rules, with the corresponding punishment. Although this could help in making the Metaverse more granular and enable a certain level of governance regarding privacy and security, it could lead to closed areas or "virtual ghettos," which could go against democratic principles and the respect for freedom and nondiscrimination.

Another challenge that the Metaverse needs to address is how to handle sensitive information of minors since they constitute a wide portion of increasingly sophisticated and tech-savvy digital users and a lot of Metaverse services are expected to address this population, especially (e.g., education, entertainment). They are usually less aware of the risks involved in the processing of their data. From a practical standpoint, it is often difficult to verify whether a user is a child, even in the current

Internet, and thus valid parental consent is required. Service providers in the Metaverse should accordingly review the measures they are taking to protect children's data and consider more effective verification mechanisms, other than just relying upon consent mechanisms, which could be faked. Like in the physical world, Metaverse services could benefit from features like face recognition or verbal maturity of the user to get a range of the user's age and combine it with other mechanisms to improve the reliability of protection measures for children.

Finally, designing such protection for vulnerable groups is not limited to children. Vulnerable people include not only those more likely to be susceptible to privacy violations but also those whose safety and well-being are disproportionately affected by such violations, or are likely to suffer discrimination because of information about their physical or mental disorder, race, gender, sex, class, and similar attributes. A growing number of concerns, and new solutions, is expected in relation to this subject as the Metaverse matures in the next years.

## Summary

In this chapter, we have read about many ideas concerning security in the Metaverse, summarized as follows:

- The Metaverse will manage a lot more information and personal details than the current Internet. Therefore, a lot of concerns arise regarding security and privacy.
- Until now, all space on earth has been ruled and controlled by a government. There is still no agreement, and very few models, for the governance of the virtual spaces in the Metaverse.
- Regulation is expected in the next years, either related to virtual spaces or to the protection of the avatars in the Metaverse.
- Technology makes things more difficult: AI-based avatars and deepfakes can represent a serious security issue in the Metaverse.

- Trust and accountability in the Metaverse are a matter of study regarding security: people tend to behave more irresponsibly when not directly facing others. Additionally, some groups that are less skilled in using the new technologies would be much more vulnerable to scams.
- Security policies and ethical rules must be implemented in the Metaverse. However, as a completely new space for exploration, if overprotective based on past premises that are no longer valid in the virtual world, they could hinder the development of new services and applications.

# CHAPTER 14

# When Will the Metaverse Transform Into Reality

As we have already seen, the Metaverse is based on technologies that already exist. From a theoretical point of view, it could be a reality, although only as reduced experiments. The reason is that, even when something is feasible, there is still a need to develop an ecosystem and produce and deploy some elements at a large scale to become practical. Maybe you know how to prepare cookies, and maybe you can get the ingredients very easily, but there is a huge leap before you can build a food company that can cook and sell millions of cookies around the globe.

In this chapter, we will analyze what is needed before the Metaverse is democratized, that is, accessible to all public and widely used in our daily lives.

## The Scalability Problem

Current experiments of immersive virtual rooms show that, with the current technologies regarding graphic card (GPU, or graphical processing units, technically speaking) computing performance and network bandwidth, it is possible to scale such interactive environments just to tens of participants. Even when cryptocurrency mining and the video gaming industry have multiplied the demand for high-performance GPUs, pushing performance up while keeping the devices affordable, the main problem is that, as more participants access the room, the corresponding uploading and downloading demand increases exponentially. This is because the server hosting the virtual room, either serving just as a relay or performing further content processing, must compute a 3D dynamic view for each and, each time a new user joins, more 3D moving images need to be computed for each of the other participants. As a result, the server will quickly become overloaded and stop working correctly.

*Table 14.1 Equivalence in technical requirements between 3D immersive video and regular 2D streaming*

| 3D video technology | 3D Bandwidth | Equivalent 2D streaming (TV) | 2D bandwidth |
|---|---|---|---|
| 2 x 2D 2k images, 30 fps, 8-bit color | 100 Mbps | SD (720 x 480) | 1.1 Mbps |
| 2 x 2D 4k images, 60 fps, 10-bit color | 400 Mbps | HD (1080p) | 5 Mbps |
| 2 x 3D 8K images, 120 fps, 12-bit color | 2 Gbps | 4K (2160p) | 20 Mbps |

Regarding the bandwidth requirement of Metaverse applications, we must know that, compared to traditional 2D videos, the bandwidth for transmitting the equivalent 3D videos (same resolution, same duration, same color depth ...) is huge, as shown in Table 14.1.

We can see the bandwidth of the Internet connection to make the Metaverse work at home or on our mobile devices is around 100 times larger than conventional streaming videos. Although there are many homes with higher bandwidth than that, the problem resides on the server side, as it is now impossible to provide such bandwidth to a large number of users from the same network node, hosting the virtual room.

## The Need for New Devices

The second challenge to making the Metaverse mainstream is accessibility. Today's Internet access does not need specific devices. Smartphones, tablets, and computers are found in every home. To access the Metaverse, users are required to wear 3D headsets for better interaction in the virtual world. The problem with them is not only the need for anyone to acquire a new relatively expensive device but also that headsets greatly limit accessibility, in the sense that many applications are not possible, and headsets can only be used in controlled physical environments (normally in a clear space indoors). Some vendors are making efforts to produce new interfacing devices for accessing the Metaverse, like more standard and appealing glasses, contact lenses, and even access without wearing any additional device (Park and Kim 2022).

Moreover, we only tend to think of the Metaverse as a combination of spatial audio and 3D video inputs, but interaction techniques need to incorporate the other senses, like feeling, smelling, and even tasting, like what we do in the physical world (Dionisio and Gilbert 2013). This path is still in the very starting experimental phase.

Yet another issue related to accessibility is the interoperability across different implementations of the Metaverse, especially when users move from one platform to another. As an emerging technology, we expect that the large technology vendors will provide their own devices for certain platforms as we have experienced in the past. The user experience should be seamless without any interruption and let anyone access all contents in the Metaverse, but this probably will not be so from the beginning.

## Connecting the Physical Reality

The Metaverse will serve as a bridge between the physical and digital worlds. In fact, as we have seen throughout this book, the Metaverse can be understood as a networked world parallel to the real world. But this is not fully true. Both worlds will interact in certain circumstances where data produced in the physical world will feed Metaverse applications or information repositories, and actions taken in the Metaverse by users or virtual elements will translate into physical actions in reality.

Let's see an illustrative example: A Metaverse application could replicate the actual physical weather conditions on a specific beach to simulate that environment in the virtual space. For that, physical data (temperature, light, rain, clouds, wind, etc.) should be measured in the real world and then fed to the Metaverse app. In the same way, the same app could have access to the heating and air conditioner systems of the user's home as well as to special fans, to emulate the current temperature and wind in that beach in the user's physical room.

Although more variables are digitally measured in our physical world every day, the requirements to provide truly immersive experiences in the Metaverse are vast. Therefore, in the beginning, it is expected that Metaverse apps provide vague or poor immersive experiences, just enough to deliver some appointed services through minimum viable products (MVPs). For instance, the Metaverse shopping experience could be limited to just floating 3D representations of the objects, but we would not be able to *catch* them and check how much they weigh, feel their texture and consistency, and so on.

The effort to connect the physical reality with the Metaverse bidirectionally is enormous and it is thus expected to be continuous effort for years. This effort will consist on two evolutional paths: the first, the digitization of the whole reality (measuring and recording *everything*), and second, the development of software and methods that can process such vast amount of data to provide new experiences and applications to users in the Metaverse.

## Smart Cities and Sensors Everywhere

"Smart city" is a concept used to define a complex and interconnected system that applies digital technologies to manage the typical process in an urban area. These technologies can be applied to nearly everything, from the public and private transport systems to the efficient use of energy or water resources, including civil protection plans, or socioeconomic aspects, such as the efficient and better use of public spaces, or the communication of incidents to inhabitants and visitors.

A smart city detects the needs of its citizens and reacts by transforming the interactions of citizens with the systems and elements of public service into knowledge. The final goal of smart city services is to provide real-time solutions to citizens' problems or demands, or even anticipate what may happen.

As you may have guessed, the deployment of smart city services implies installing sensors to measure different variables in the city: smart water or electricity counters, cameras, weather sensors, noise sensors, traffic sensors, police, ambulance, and firefighting officers' and vehicles' GPS location sensors, people density sensors, sewer draining sensors, air pollution sensors, sensors, sensors, and more sensors. All this information is now used twofold: first, to feed large databases that can show trends on different aspects such as pollution or noise, and second, to provide real-time information to take actions, like sending a patrolling vehicle if unusual traffic congestion is detected or make recommendations to citizens if pollution or pollen has reached the maximum recommended threshold for certain activities like running.

This is a trend that started first in larger cities and was then adopted by many other towns or urban areas. It is expected to remain for the next coming years, with much more sensors deployed worldwide each year. And this is needed to develop new Metaverse applications as well because, as seen before, sensors are the basis to digitize information from the real world and feed it in the Metaverse and also because the databases associated to smart city services will greatly help develop virtual models for the Metaverse about many aspects of our daily life.

## Developing New Useful Applications

Developing software for the Metaverse implies a lot of work and study as there are still few resources to learn and many possibilities that have not been discovered yet. There is not enough information for practical details to make complex and realistic implementations (e.g., object selection, conditional actions, user storyboards with scene flow, teleportation between scenes, movement, and dialogue). When such new technology or technological ecosystem is born, developers communities appear, to help individual developers codevelop without designing the entire system. There are some commercial collaborative platforms like Roblox already successfully running, as well as open-source ones like Unity.

This is crucial for the massive adoption of the Metaverse. Although we see some early attempts to make *translations* of some applications to the Metaverse, most of them will seem only attractive to early adopters of the Metaverse, as very little or no added value will be in there (e.g., watching YouTube videos in a virtual theater). An important leap will be done once new genuine Metaverse applications are developed, delivering services and experiences that are impossible out of the Metaverse, such as trying clothes or accessories directly on your body, your ear, or your wrist. Anyway, we can expect some years before appealing and impressive true Metaverse applications are available and widely adopted.

## Fighting Against Multiple Metaverses

We saw in the first chapter of this book that the Metaverse, like any technology that aims to become globally extended, is decentralized by nature. Decentralized technology includes Blockchain technology, distributed storage, distributed computing, and so on. There are many companies now providing *their own metaverse*, the most famous being Meta. Honestly speaking, these solutions are not the Metaverse but isolated VR spaces. We can make a comparison with the incipient isolated computer networks in the 1970s (most of them to connect bank branches) and the Internet we know, where everything is connected to everything.

What made the Internet possible was two things: one, the common use of some communication protocols (namely, TCP/IP) between all organizations worldwide; and the other, what is technically called a "discovery tool," mostly known as "search engines" (e.g., Google, Bing). In the context of the Metaverse, an urgent problem to be solved is how to effectively discover and allocate resources. Researchers are constantly exploring resource management strategies to provide the foundation for the implementation of the Metaverse, for example, a resource search and discovery algorithm for heterogeneous environments, or a dynamic resource allocation framework to synchronize the Metaverse with services and data connected to external sources and the physical reality.

However, we will likely see some private initiatives providing isolated metaverse-like services before we reach a maturity state where we can enjoy a Google-like search engine to surf between the different virtual spaces and applications in the Metaverse. Furthermore, in the Metaverse, our avatar and some spatial context is crucial for many services, and there is still no definite answer about how developers should use common protocols or standards to let us use the same avatar and contextual information (e.g., the configuration of the physical room we use to connect to the Metaverse, the type of devices we have) in different applications.

Thus, as a virtual world closely connected to reality and with a complex multidimensional nature, it is necessary to establish standards for the Metaverse. Furthermore, the compatibility and standardization issues of the Metaverse are not only about issues between the metaverses created by different companies but also about connecting the Metaverse and the real world. For instance, currency compatibility and circulation issues, and handling of legal disputes. Figure 14.1 shows the complex technological and functional ecosystem that needs to be managed to get an integrated experience in the Metaverse. In the beginning, a full degree of freedom is expected for any company developing metaverse-like applications. The more time standards are not set, the more difficult future interoperability between applications and services will be.

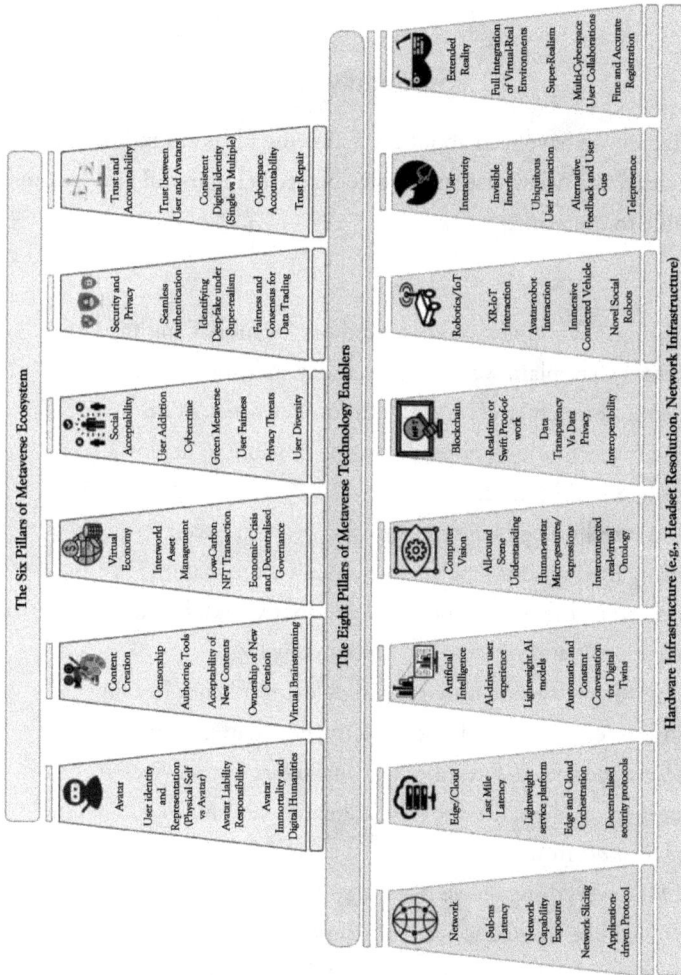

*Figure 14.1 Enabling technologies and functional components of the Metaverse*

Source: Lee et al. 2021.

In conclusion, although there are some initiatives toward building metaverse applications, there is an urgent need to approve and follow some standards for interoperability between them and the integration of external information sources. Otherwise, we could see in the next years the quick rise and fall of the Metaverse before a future second opportunity arrives.

## Summary

In this chapter, we have read about the following ideas around barriers or challenges that the Metaverse must solve before being useful and becoming available to everyone:

- 3D images and virtual spaces require far more computing power than plain websites used today. Additionally, they demand much larger bandwidth on networks. With today's technology, it would not be possible to deploy a generalized Metaverse.
- Input technologies (gesture devices, wearables, etc.) are just being used in some applications. Much more maturity is needed before they become widely adopted and, furthermore, ergonomic and comfortable for our daily lives.
- The Metaverse will only remain as VR if it is not heavily interlaced with the physical reality. For that, a lot more smart sensors, IoT technology, and smart city services are needed, to digitalize the physical reality and make it *actionable* from the Metaverse.
- Once everything above is more or less ready, more time will still be needed to let vendors develop new applications and services in the Metaverse, not simply "translating" the current ones.
- In the fight for conquering the Metaverse, the initial phase will find a lot of isolated metaverses. In time, they will converge and consolidate until we can enjoy a unified Metaverse.

# CHAPTER 15

# Potential Side Effects of the Metaverse

The Metaverse will bring about a new kind of social relationship that integrates online and offline interactions. The emergence of the Metaverse will not replace physical social relationships with virtual social relationships but will add new forms—sometimes preferred—of communication between individuals. The massive adoption of the Metaverse in our daily lives will therefore bring new issues related to human communications, emotions, and social conventions.

In this chapter, the most relevant potential side effects of the changes introduced by the Metaverse in society are analyzed (summarized in Figure 15.1). All of them take into consideration the experience acquired with the generalized adoption of social media and personal connectivity. However, in the same way as what occurred with social media, some other future side effects that are still unknown could also appear.

## Cyber-Syndrome

Cyber-syndrome is a set of physical, social, and mental disorders that affect human beings due to the misusage of technology or the excessive interaction with cyberspace. Cyber-syndrome is closely related to four behaviors (Beard and Wolf 2001):

1. Excessive interaction with cyberspace, which means connecting to cyberspace without limits or in no reasonable way. In other words, connecting to cyberspace is not inherently misguided, but the line between normal use and addiction fibs where a positive or neutral use crosses into negative territory.

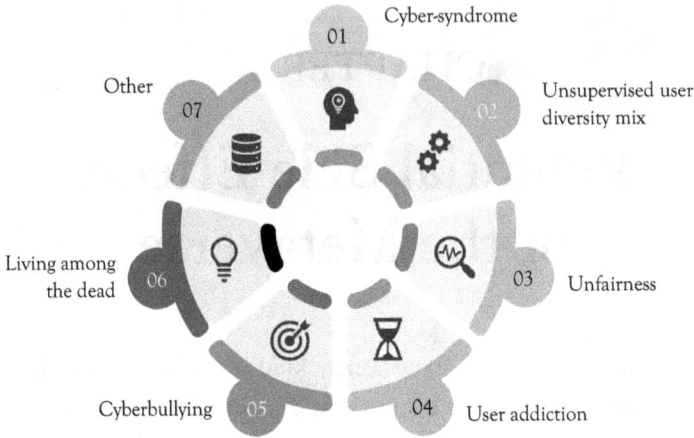

*Figure 15.1 Potential side effects of the Metaverse*

2. State of lack, where an unpleasant sensation is felt when there are rules or a reduction in the frequency of interaction with cyberspace, such as sadness, anxiety, irritability, anger, or boredom when access to technology is not possible.

3. Tolerance in addition to the excessive interaction with cyberspace. Tolerance means the need to increase quantities or durations to achieve the same effects in a short time, like purchasing new equipment and apps to increasing hours spent in front of terminals, which will lead to complete or partial ignorance of the surrounding environment.

4. External consequences, such as loss of interest in previous hobbies or meaningful relationships, work or marriage problems, and spending more time plugged in cyberspace rather than going out with friends or joining family activities.

With the continuous development of interactive methods, electronic devices have become smaller and more portable. The streamlining of equipment and the seamless and addictive design of many apps and digital services make people spend more and more time on the Internet. Bringing this situation to the Metaverse, which is closely connected with the real world, can blur the frontiers between virtual and real, and the high degree of immersion of Metaverse applications and services could worsen the problem of cyber-syndrome, making many people prefer the VR to the physical one.

Finally, as the Metaverse becomes commonplace in our daily lives, user addiction will be a crucial issue. People may rely on the Metaverse to escape from the real world, just as described in the novel *Snow Crash*, published in 1992 by Neal Stephenson.

Without submitting to a fully technological determinist resignation, it does seem inevitable that as workers, educators, learners, and social beings, we will increasingly encounter VR and invitations to meet in the Metaverse. As the Metaverse becomes more widely accessed, it offers an exciting arena for human–computer interaction and computer-supported collaborative work. But there are inherent risks. The mass adoption of social media as the global norm for technology-mediated socialization has given us a foretaste of the surveillant possibilities of capitalism to appropriate value from users' data in the Metaverse. The economic, environmental, and other types of pressures to adopt VR—enter the Metaverse—and expand digitization to all daily activities and objects are enormous. We cannot precisely measure what health, social, or economic impacts the Metaverse will have on people in the coming years, but we are sure it will profoundly change the behavior of society and human interactions.

## Unsupervised User Diversity Mix

As stated in a visionary design of human–city interaction (Lee et al. 2020), the design of mobile AR/MR user interaction in citywide urban should consider various stakeholders. Similarly, the Metaverse should be inclusive to everyone in the community, regardless of race, gender, age, religion, and so on. In the Metaverse, any content can eventually appear, and there is no guarantee to ensure it is appropriate to the intended audience. We can size this problem by better transposing the problem in physical reality to the virtual space: in the physical world, different areas are designed for different audiences. For instance, parks have a space for children, stairs have a side ramp for wheelchair users, nightclubs have age restrictions, and so on. Doing the same in the Metaverse is *theoretically* possible but, given the possibility to jump from any place to another in a matter of seconds and the infinite possibilities offered by the Metaverse, where no barriers (frontiers, country regulations, etc.) exist, this task could become cumbersome.

In addition, diversity is also important when referring to showing personalized content to users. There could be some doubt about the fairness of the recommendation systems to minimize biased content and thus impact users' behaviors and decision making. The contents in virtual worlds can lead to higher acceptance by delivering factors of enjoyment, emotional involvement, excitement, and other similar feelings. Where to put the limits in the Metaverse is still not determined, which could give rise to a serious ethical issue with devastating side effects for citizens.

## Unfairness

Numerous virtual worlds will be built in the Metaverse, and perhaps every virtual world has its separate rules to govern users' behaviors and activities. As such, the efforts of managing and maintaining such virtual worlds would be enormous. We expect that autonomous agents, supported by AI, will engage in the role of governance in virtual worlds, to alleviate the demands of manual workload. It is important to pinpoint that the autonomous agents in virtual worlds rely on ML to react to the continuous changes of virtual objects and avatars. It is well-known that no model can perfectly describe the real-world instance, and similarly, an unfair or biased model could systematically harm the user experience in the Metaverse or even be contrary to the common sense about what would be expected in the physical reality. The biased services could put certain user groups in disadvantageous positions or even cause harm.

We can see a similarity on social networks, where just summarizing user-generated texts by algorithmic approaches can make some social groups underrepresented. In contrast, fairness-preserving summarization algorithms can produce overall high-quality services across social groups. It would be expected that Metaverse designers, considering the Metaverse as a virtual society, should include algorithmic fairness as the core value of the Metaverse designs and accordingly keep procedural justice when employing algorithms and computer agents to take managerial and governance roles. However, this requires a high degree of transparency to the users and outcome control mechanisms, which is not guaranteed. We are now facing a "censorship school of thought" related to social media content, where many people think that it is fair that a private company uses opaque policies to ban certain content, while others see this as an outrage to individual liberty. The translation of such open issues to the Metaverse will produce a much larger effect on citizens' reactions, given the higher engagement of the Metaverse with emotions and senses.

In conclusion, the relevance of user perceptions to the fairness of such ML methods is crucial for fairness *perception*. However, leaning to perceived fairness could fall into another trap of outcoming favorability bias.

## User Addiction

Excessive use of digital environments may be considered an addiction. It would be an important issue when the Metaverse becomes the most prevalent venue for people to spend their time interacting with digital services. In the worst scenario, users may leverage the Metaverse to help them *escape* from the real world, which is a psychological disorder called escapism. Some research has already found evidence of addictions to various virtual cyberspaces or digital platforms such as social networks, mobile applications, smartphones, VR, AR, and other digital technologies.

User addictions to cyberspace could lead to psychological issues and mental disorders, such as depression, loneliness, and user aggression. The Covid-19 pandemic has prompted a paradigm shift from face-to-face meetings or social gatherings to various virtual ways and recent research has indicated that the prolonged use of such virtual meetings and gatherings can create abusive use or addiction to the Internet.

Therefore, the question is whether the Metaverse will bring its users to the next level of addiction. We can already foresee the potential behavior changes by reviewing the existing AR/VR platforms. First, VR Chat, known as a remarkable example of Metaverse virtual worlds, can be considered a pilot example of addiction to the Metaverse. Additionally, VR researchers have also studied the relationship between addiction to VR, root causes, and corresponding treatments. Also, AR games like Pokémon Go could lead to a behavior change in massive players, such as spending behaviors, group-oriented actions in urban areas, and dangerous or risky actions in the real world. Such behavior changes, if resulting from addiction, could lead to difficult-to-solve impacts on society.

A psychological approach to user addiction explains that the Metaverse can become the extended self of a user, including the person's mind, body, physical possessions, family, friends, and affiliation groups. This extension of nearly the whole user's life in the Metaverse encourages him or her to explore more and more virtual environments and pursue rewards, perhaps in an endless reward–feedback loop. We must highlight that the issues of addiction to immersive environments in the Metaverse are expected to become much worse than in any other means (e.g., social media) due to the super-realism that allows users to experience activities highly resembling the real world and deeply influencing several senses at a time. Also, highly realistic virtual environments enable people to try things that are impossible in real life (e.g., an event that is immoral, showing racism, etc.). It could happen that such more permissive environments, which may also give the impression of privacy to users by physically being at home, can further exacerbate the addictions, for instance, extending the usage time or creating stronger emotions.

## Cyberbullying

Cyberbullying or cyber-harassment is a form of bullying or harassment using electronic means. Cyberbullying and cyber-harassment are also known as online bullying. Bullying behavior can include posting rumors, false information, threats, sexual remarks, the victim's personal information, or pejorative labels. Currently, cyberbullying frequently occurs on social networks as the most extended means for digital communication, but the Metaverse will become a gigantic cyberspace. As such, another social high-concern threat is cyberbullying in the Metaverse. It is possible that, according to the usual practice today, the Metaverse could not control cyberbullying when becoming mainstream, and authorities will request to shut down some virtual worlds.

But this will be the first attempt to solve a problem without success. Considering the almost infinite number of virtual worlds in the Metaverse, the next approach will be cyberbullying detection driven by algorithms or ML methods. The fairness of such approaches will become the crucial factors in delivering perceived fairness to the users in the Metaverse. After identifying any cyberbullying cases, mitigation solutions such as care and support, virtual social support, and self-disclosure, would be effectively deployed in virtual environments.

However, recognizing cyberbullying in the game-alike environment the Metaverse represents is far more complicated than in current social networks, where interaction is sequential and plain (a post after another is placed in a timeline). For instance, users' misbehavior can be vague and difficult to identify such as a smile, a glance, or a whisper, very similar to what happens in the real world. Similarly, 3D virtual worlds inside the Metaverse could further complicate the scenarios and hence make the detection of cyberbullying difficult at scale. Therefore, citizens will probably need to coexist with a higher dose of cyberbullying, and we still do not know the psychological and sociological consequences of this.

## Living Among the Dead

If we analyze Metaverse avatar dynamics, we can find another relevant social issue that comes from their acceptability under certain circumstances. As we know, avatars can be genuine creations or digital copies of the users they represent. We have also seen how avatars could work semi autonomously or even fully autonomously when the user is offline. Then, once a user passes away, what is the acceptability of the user's family members, relatives, or friends to his or her avatar? Should it be legally linked, somehow, to make it disappear as well from the virtual world or not? With time, as AI makes avatars autonomously behave like their real owners, this question could also shape the future of a *digital humanity* in the Metaverse, composed of virtual objects and avatars that could become immortal, as separate entities from the real world. What implications will it have? Let's suppose that the Metaverse existed when Albert Einstein was still alive, and today we can find his own avatar still living in the Metaverse. Would it not be reasonable to include him in the most relevant research groups to further investigate the universe regarding the theory of relativity? Maybe we—future generations, for sure—will have to deal with such circumstances and make decisions regarding the virtual immortality of living personas and, by extension, any human being.

## Other Side Effects

First, social acceptability to the devices connecting people with the Metaverse needs further research, especially about the acceptability of the public to such devices, for example, mobile AR/VR headsets. Some questions like the safety of mobile headsets or AR glasses when moving outdoors or driving could negatively impact the reputation of those wearing these devices, slowing or limiting the adoption of the Metaverse, especially for the development of certain services. Much likely, device manufacturers will evolve their current designs to other more friendly, lightweight, and discreet devices. Or, like what happened with other devices like smartwatches and even smartphones, there could be a trend to exhibit extravagant large devices to differentiate from those citizens who are "technologically obsolete."

Another expected social effect in the adoption of the Metaverse is what has already happened regarding social media and age. Many studies conclude that social networks are used distinctly by different generations. For instance, generation Z prefers Instagram, Snapchat, and TikTok over Facebook. Rather, Facebook retains more users from Gen X and Y. We can expect the same generational segregation in the Metaverse virtual worlds.

Moving away from social aspects and centering on the environment, the Metaverse, as a gigantic digital world, will be supported by countless computational devices. They will generate huge energy consumption and pollution. Given that the Metaverse should not deprive future generations, designers of Metaverse infrastructure and applications should not neglect the design considerations from the perspective of green computing. Eco-friendliness and environmental responsibility could impact the user affection and attitude toward the Metaverse, and perhaps the number of active users and opposers. Therefore, sourcing and building the Metaverse with data analytics on the basis of sustainability indices would become necessary, and we expect some disequilibrium between countries more concerned about environmental sustainability (e.g., the European Union) and others.

# Ethical Implications

The Metaverse gives people the opportunity to have new identities. It creates a new free space for our daily life and activities. At the same time, because of the augmented options it provides compared to physical reality, it contains more complicated social relationships. As a next-generation network, the Metaverse must control and constrain users' behavior and establish clear ethical and moral norms to maintain a good and orderly ecological environment, as shown in Chapter 7.

The ethical and moral problems of the Metaverse refer to the phenomena that arise due to the eventual absence and confusion of the corresponding moral norms, which conflict with society's ethical norms. Like in current Internet applications, some ethical and moral issues in the Metaverse are related to the integrity or fraud when publishing and disseminating false information, the problem of unfavorable atmosphere, and the infringement of intellectual property rights. But, more importantly, when the brain's information, potentially including consciousness, can be edited, stored, and copied as digital data, the role of ethics will become the essence. Therefore, the supervision of the Metaverse should be strengthened, and new regulations should be formulated and updated, according to the new technological possibilities and their impact on human rights and societal behavior.

# Summary

In this chapter, we have read about the following ideas associated with the potential side effects of the Metaverse:

- The psychological effects of the Metaverse will be deeper than those of current social media. This is sustained by the fact that it touches more senses in the organism and more vividly.
- The cyber-syndrome is characterized by connecting to cyberspace excessively (even with no reason behind it), with a sense of lack when unconnected and increasing tolerance in time (the need for more to experience the same effect).

- A diversity mix of users present in a virtual space in the Metaverse without supervision can represent a threat for minors and minorities.
- The speed of digital technologies and the easy "tweaking" of some rules or algorithms can result in an unfair space where some groups are underrepresented or where people follow some *generalized* ideas just to not be banned or criticized.
- User addiction in the Metaverse could have severe consequences. People abandoning their physical lives to enjoy their virtual ones could suffer from illness to death if body senses were too obfuscated with artificial feelings, so basic vital processes are disrupted.
- Cyberbullying will increase in the Metaverse as a richer extension of digital socialization.
- The extended use of AI in the Metaverse and the promising developments toward digital twins could raise an ethical question regarding whether deceased people's avatars should remain alive in the Metaverse. The social implications of this scenario, where *nobody dies in the Metaverse*, is still unknown.

# CHAPTER 16

# Some Revelations About the Future

## Digital Twins, Digital Consciousness, Transhumanism, Immortality

So far in our Metaverse journey, we have a lot of *can be, would,* and *expected.* This is because the Metaverse underlying technologies are still being developed, and more news is coming out every day. As more companies start developing and testing new features and releasing information, the Metaverse gains a better tangible grounded side. In this chapter, we discuss what the future holds not only for the Metaverse but also for us as a society because of the introduction of the Metaverse and what we can expect to see in the next years.

### Digital Twins

Digital twins are digital clones with high integrity and fidelity to their physical counterpart entities or systems. Digital twins do not only remain as a digital copy of a physical object but also keep interacting with the physical world, in the form of *synchronization* between the physical and the digital object, or just staying as a separate digital duplicate that can interact with physical tools or other physical objects. Digital twins can be used to provide classification, recognition, prediction, and determination services for their physical entities.

Strictly speaking, digital twins are just one method for object or system digitization. Depending on the possibility of automating the digitization process and to close the feedback loop between the digital object and the physical one, the three methods are shown in Figure 16.1: digital model, digital shadow, and digital twin.

A **digital model** is just a digital replication of a physical entity. As we can see in Figure 16.1, there is no automated interaction between the digital object (in the Metaverse) and the physical world. The digital model is normally obtained by manually measuring the physical entity or using mathematic formulas and calculations to design the model. This method has existed since long ago and has been extensively used in simulations and mockups, for instance.

A **digital shadow** is the automated digital representation of a physical entity. If the physical entity changes, its digital shadow automatically changes, accordingly. This method is being currently developed for many applications, especially in health care, to obtain accurate 3D live representations of body parts for diagnosis in telemedicine.

Last, in the case of a **digital twin**, the object in the Metaverse and that in the physical world can influence each other. Any change in any of them will have an immediate effect on the other one. For that, it is necessary to automate the interaction between both entities. Deep learning has proven to be a highly effective technique to automatically extract information from the large amount of complex data needed to build a digital twin and represent it in various kinds of applications without the need for manual work.

**Deep learning** is a technique based on unsupervised neural networks, a digital architecture that emulates the working principle of neurons in a brain. Like our brains, a deep learning system needs to be first trained with sample data, so it can *learn* patterns, inferences, and rules to get to conclusions. Thus, to build a digital twin of an object or a system,

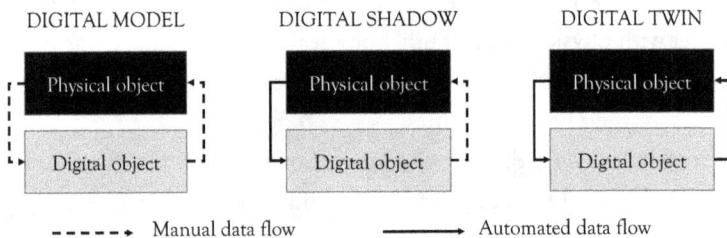

*Figure 16.1 Methods for object or system digitization*

training is first needed, which normally takes a digital model previously designed (e.g., if we want to get a digital twin of a human hand, an engineer first designs a digital model of the hand with its joints, allowed movements, dimensions, etc.). In the training phase, data from both worlds, the Metaverse, and the physical reality, are fused together in training–testing cycles. If the testing results meet the expected results and the accuracy requirement, the autonomous system is ready to be deployed. In the implementation phase, real-time data from both worlds will also be used to further train and improve the coherence between the physical object or system and the digital twin.

Once the digital twin of an object is ready to be used, another relevant technology that can be useful for further exploitation is **additive manufacturing**. Additive manufacturing is commonly known as "3D printing." It consists of producing a physical part of different materials (plastic, metal, concrete, etc.) from a digital model. Digital twins directly connect virtual spaces with the physical world. Human users could subsequently start content creation in the digital twins. Accordingly, the digitally created or updated content could be reflected in physical environments through additive manufacturing. It is important to highlight that such editing in the digital twins does not need to be *additions*. They can consist of *changes* like cutting, bumping, moving, and so on. For instance, in remote surgery, a surgeon could be effectively working on the digital twin of the patient's organ while a robot could be replicating such changes to the actual patient's organ remotely.

Although we cannot accurately predict how the Metaverse will eventually impact our physical surroundings, we see the existing MR prototypes enclose some specific goals, such as pursuing scenes of realism, bringing a sense of presence, and creating empathetic virtual spaces that replicate physical ones. Considering this, we can, however, predict that reality and the Metaverse will merge in a blurred MR at a certain level over time, so we could hardly differentiate when we are playing in the Metaverse or in the physical reality in some moments.

As we see, digital twins can be the real foundation of the Metaverse, where digital objects will behave similarly to physical ones. The interactions in the Metaverse can be used to improve the physical systems, converging in a disruptive innovation path to enhance the overall life experience.

# Holography

A concept that is closely tied to digital twins is holography. Holography is the art of recording and reproducing an accurate three-dimensional image of an object (or a person) by optical means. It is the result of the combination of computer technology and optic technology. We are used to seeing holographic images in science fiction movies like Star Trek or Star Wars, where a 3D image of a person speaking to others appears in a room in the form of emerging light coming from a small device on the floor or on the table. This futuristic technology, that is real and extensively tested at present, uses the phenomenon called *coherent light interference* to record the amplitude information and phase information of the light wave and obtain all the information of the object, including shape, size, and other features. Although the physical principle is a little hard to explain using nontechnical terms, we can figure it as a device producing crossing laser rays that are invisible to human eyes (like those in our TV remote or radio waves), but that become visible if one crosses another in a specific point. By repeating this ray superposition millions of times in the air, even using different light colors, a device can picture a complete 3D object, visible to the naked eye at different angles, without the need to wear any portable device. This technology further blurs the boundary between the physical and the virtual worlds, creating a solid foundation for the real realization of the Metaverse.

# Digital Consciousness

Consciousness is a concept whose definition is made only at a theoretical level. Nobody knows clearly what consciousness is, although all of us feel conscious most of the time. When trying to describe consciousness from a technological perspective, a widely accepted approach proposed in 2017 (Dehaene 2021) divides consciousness into two dimensions: C1—subconsciousness and C2—actual consciousness.

**Subconsciousness** contains information and a huge range of processes in the brain, where most human intelligence lies. Subconsciousness enables us to choose a chess move or spot a face. Researchers believe that this type of consciousness has already been developed in digital systems in the form of artificial intelligence (AI) algorithms and machine learning (ML) methods, especially deep learning, as seen before.

**Actual consciousness** contains and monitors information about oneself, split into two groups:

- The ability to keep a huge range of thoughts (knowledge, ideas, and beliefs) at once, all accessible to other parts of the brain, making abilities like long-term planning or creativity possible. This group is starting to be developed in digital systems, being the most challenging question to know how the human brain works to combine such a vast amount of information to produce something useful in a short period.
- The ability to obtain and process information about ourselves, which allows us to do things like reflecting on mistakes or questioning what the purpose of our life is. This part is not implemented on digital systems, although some attempts have been made as a "fake consciousness" based on preprogrammed rules or assumptions. The problem with implementing this type of consciousness is that, indeed, we do not still know how it works in the human brain, so we cannot replicate or recreate something that is unknown.

It seems that actual consciousness is driven by billions of neurons that bind together information from subconsciousness, following stochastic probability like in quantum mechanics. But before actual consciousness is possible, another subconscious phenomenon is needed, called **awareness**. Awareness is the ability to know, perceive, feel, recognize, and act on events. A brick does not have any perception or feeling of anything, so it is unaware of what happens to it and its environment. But all animals are aware *to an extent*. For instance, a gazelle runs close to its pack when it feels threatened by a lion to minimize the probability of being the prey. On the contrary, a fly is not aware of the enormous risk of death when being in a bedroom with people inside.

Awareness seems to be directly related to the number of neurons and connections between them in the brain. Regarding digital consciousness, which is the way machines would behave like human beings in the sense of feeling, reflecting, and believing, this discovery about awareness can be a very good start: we only need more powerful computers to emulate millions of neurons—just a matter of time, as everybody knows. Therefore, the main assumption taken here is that once superintelligence emerges, understood as AI evolved into much more powerful systems that can surpass human intelligence in many topics, it will be possible that, at some stage, it will come up with conscious systems.

The question is: once we perform a big share of our daily activities in the Metaverse and digital consciousness can be a reality, there will be many digital entities (virtual *people* only *alive* inside the Metaverse) whose behavior would be impossible to differentiate from a human's. Furthermore, virtual entities are built on software, so they can be eternal, as they are not affected by the biological cycles, and their *digital neurons* can work several orders of magnitude faster than humans', using one ten-thousandth of the amount of energy used by a biological neuron. You can guess that, in a very short period, progressing exponentially, AI and digital consciousness will become dominant on earth.

## Brain–Computer Interfaces (BCIs)

Digital consciousness is not all we will see soon. BCIs are another developing technology that encodes and decodes brain signals in the process of brain activity by accurately identifying the small electric pulses used by neurons to process information and stimuli. BCIs can connect human thoughts and sensing experiences with the digital world by decoding individual brain signals into information recognized by software applications. This will represent a direct plug of our brains to the Metaverse in less than we think.

BCI technology can be divided into three types: invasive, semi-invasive, and noninvasive. Figure 16.2 represents a portion of the head, including the brain, the cerebrospinal fluid, the skull, and the skin. Different technological solutions are shown, from noninvasive ones on the left (near-infrared, NIR; conventional EEG, electroencephalogram) to the most invasive ones on the right end. The invasiveness level refers to the need for surgery to implant electrodes into the cerebral cortex or nearby. BCI is currently used in experiments to treat severe brain trauma

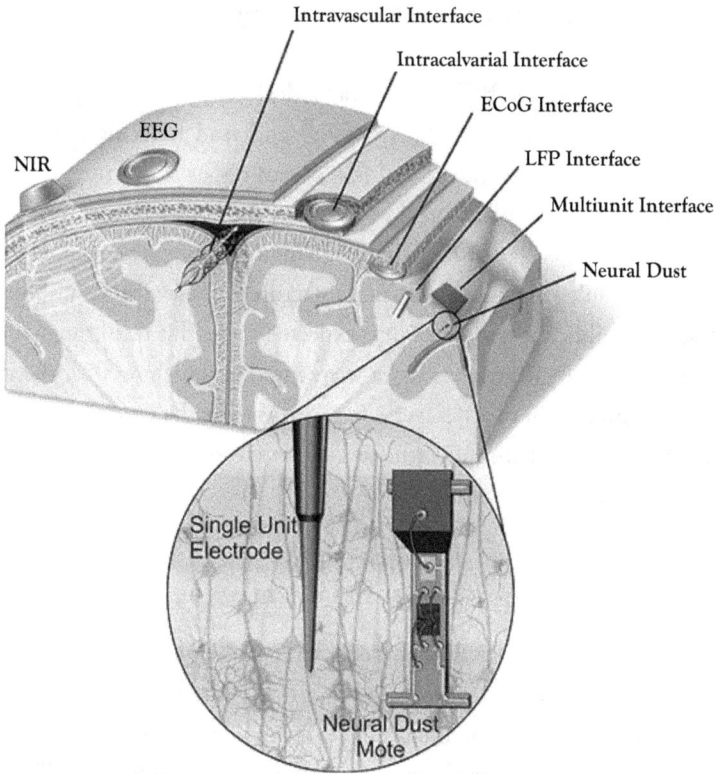

**Figure 16.2** *Different technologies used to build brain–computer interfaces*

Source: Leuthardt et al. 2021.

or brain diseases, and apart from the requirement of complex surgery, the long-term stability of these systems is not yet fully studied.

Semi-invasive BCIs require the implantation of electrodes into the cranial cavity but outside the cerebral cortex. Normally, semi-invasive techniques require electrodes with a small needle that probes brain signals with a level of accuracy. These techniques are also experimental and are intended mostly to avoid the secondary effects and potential damage to the brain caused by invasive techniques. While invasive techniques are not expected to be part of the Metaverse ecosystem, at least in the next years, semi-invasive techniques are being explored by some groups, like the famous Elon Musk's company Neuralink, which is developing a chip implant with several wired electrodes to connect the brain to digital devices. This can be the kickstart of transhumanism, which will be described next.

Lastly, noninvasive BCIs are wearable devices that are just placed on the scalp (headsets or helmets, normally) and read EEG signals. Noninvasive methods avoid the safety risks of surgery or skin prick, but the granularity of signal collection is low, that is, the ability to measure neuronal activity *in high resolution*. There are many noninvasive BCI devices already available, including mass-manufactured ones with very limited measuring abilities at low prices. It is expected to see this technology soon implemented on VR headsets to let users interact somehow with the virtual environments in the Metaverse (e.g., measuring the user's emotion or reaction to a virtual stimulus, the level of attention, and more complex things like mentally speaking).

## Transhumanism

According to Britannica Encyclopedia, transhumanism is a social and philosophical movement devoted to promoting the research and development of robust human-enhancement technologies. Such technologies would augment or increase human sensory reception, emotive ability, or cognitive capacity, as well as radically improve human health and extend human lifespans. Such modifications resulting from the addition of biological or physical technologies would be more or less permanent and integrated into the human body.

The term *transhumanism* was coined by the English biologist and philosopher Julian Huxley in his 1957 essay of the same name. Huxley referred principally to improving the human condition through social and cultural change, not through technological devices. However, this term has been readopted recently to define the transhumanist movement, an increasing group of people who believe that the future of mankind is evolving to cyborgs, that is, adding robotic parts and artificial devices or substances to our bodies to become half humans, half robots.

The Metaverse can be a gigantic driver toward transhumanism. The same way people adopted smartphones for the vast number of applications that such small devices can provide, including security, orientation, a camera, instant communication, and other features, the Metaverse will be highly appealing to people when new applications and services are there. Sooner or later, some people will start using wearables, tattoos, and ultimately implants to avoid the unpleasant hand devices or VR helmets required today. Even some applications related to health and security will encourage their users to do that to measure their movement, vital signs, and so on.

In parallel, the advancements in robotics will provide robotic arms and legs, exoskeletons, artificial eyes and ears, and many other things that will help people with related disabilities to have a better life. Nevertheless, most of these devices may become popular on time and be massively produced for regular people that just want to have some "superpowers" (e.g., stronger arms or legs, the ability to see in the infrared spectrum, etc.). The combination of robotic developments and digital wearable devices will provide us with a large portfolio to enhance our senses and human skills. Just one step further will be needed to find people embracing the substitution of their own members and organs with artificial ones that provide enhanced performance and, who knows, even deciding to physically die and live only as a virtual life in the Metaverse.

This obscure future may be far in time, but it is one of our possible fates.

## Immortality

Death has always been disturbing humans. While animals just live their lives, our ability to think about the future makes us reflect on death and try to keep it as far from us as possible, except for some true adventurers. Immortality normally sounds good to most people, and the Metaverse can have a word to say about immortality. In the Metaverse, everything is natively digital or digitized from the physical world, and digital means the possibility to be nondegrading, as we know from music and movies, for instance, when compared to their analog equivalents.

What would happen if we could make an exact digital twin of our brain? Consciousness is supposed to be there, together with our deepest thoughts, beliefs, memory, and feelings. Is our soul also there? Could all that be copied to an exact digital model in the Metaverse? Initially, the digital twin would be synchronized with our brain so that we could be an instant in the physical reality and the next in the Metaverse. But what if we decide in that situation to leave our physical body and keep our brain, with a virtual body, just in the Metaverse? Would not we be immortals there?

Furthermore, given that scenario, why could making a physical clone of our body at the age of our preference and then resynchronizing its brain to be a copy of our digital brain in the Metaverse not be possible? We would become immortals not only in the Metaverse but also in the physical world.

You may think that these thoughts belong to science fiction movies, but I encourage you to search in Google Scholar (a large open database of scientific works) for the word "immortality" just filtering to the current year, and you will see thousands of articles studying different techniques to achieve immortal tissues and other questions related to making our presence in this world forever. The industry of immortality is just emerging today.

## Summary

In this chapter, we have read about the future. The most relevant ideas are as follows:

- Many organizations are working toward building digital twins of physical entities (even human organs). A digital twin is an accurate digital model that is *synchronized* with its associated physical entity.
- Traditional digital models are manually made. When we automatically generate a digital model from a physical entity, we call it a "digital shadow."
- If, when modifying anything in the digital shadow, these changes are automatically applied or reflected in the physical entity, then it is a "digital twin."
- Combining two innovative technologies, deep learning and additive manufacturing facilitates the development of digital twins.

- Holography is an optical technique to represent a 3D virtual object in a physical space, visible to the naked eye.
- Digital consciousness is the concept of recognizing that a machine that uses AI techniques or algorithms is conscious. The main issue related to digital consciousness is that it is still unclear what consciousness is in humans.
- BCIs are devices that can measure the activity of the brain or activate some neurons or brain locations and which are connected to computing devices or the Internet. They are currently used mostly in health care, but some initiatives are being developed to use them as input methods in the Metaverse.
- Transhumanism is a philosophy where humans can improve themselves beyond natural limitations. With the most recent technological developments, mainly BCIs, connectivity, miniaturization of computing chips, and robotics, it is becoming a potential reality.
- If a moment when a digital twin of the human brain is possible arrives, and this entails a digital twin of our souls, we could be truly immortal in the Metaverse. Maybe some people would prefer to physically die and continue living only there.

# CHAPTER 17

# And What Should I Do NOW?

Throughout this book, we have read about the Metaverse's beginnings, the different maturity states expected in the next years, how it is built, and the underlying technologies that support its architecture, especially the most innovative ones such as Blockchain, cryptocurrency, smart contracts, NFTs, VR, AR, MR, and XR.

We have also read about the possibilities that the Metaverse opens for all industries, some games and applications that are already using Metaverse technologies in an embryonic phase, what companies are already investing large sums in developing Metaverse applications and services, and how these developments can transform society for good, as we know it today.

In the last chapters, we read about potential issues associated with the paradigm shift brought by the Metaverse on current digital technologies, such as potential security and privacy issues, scalability problems, the need for new devices and sensors, and potential side effects of such an immersive technology, mostly related to the psychological condition and ethical implications.

This is the book's last chapter, and I wanted this to be the beginning of something instead of the end. So, here are some ideas about what to do next regarding the Metaverse.

## Experience the Metaverse

The best way to complete your knowledge and understanding of the concepts and possibilities mentioned in this book is to experience them personally to the extent that technology allows. If you can buy a VR headset like Meta Quest or, if money is not a problem for you, Microsoft

Hololens, go ahead! You will be able to play a lot of games and enter virtual spaces as an early adopter. Perhaps they will not be very useful for practical applications, but you will be in a much better position to follow future innovations and developments and be more *connected* to the Metaverse.

You can also do something much less expensive, even free, which is signing up in some of the early Metaverse platforms described in this book, such as Decentraland, The Sandbox, or Roblox. Maybe you can use them, not for spending your leisure time playing games or building your virtual world but for experimenting and assessing their capabilities and checking how they evolve from time to time.

## Read the News

Information on any topic is abundant nowadays. Perhaps, there is *too much* information. In fact, there is a lot of misinformation or at least worthless information about the Metaverse, as it has become a *buzzword*, frequently used for pure marketing purposes or as *clickbait* in media. For this reason, I said "read" and not "watch" in the heading; because my experience is that valuable information regarding such a technical and complex topic is typically found in written articles, papers, and books.

We have already seen that *Time* magazine has a newsletter exclusively dedicated to the Metaverse, to which you can subscribe for free (at least at the moment of writing this book).

There are also several professional groups on LinkedIn about different Metaverse topics that you can freely subscribe to as well, where you will find some drops about exciting news from time to time.

Finally, remember that you can always set a Google alert about some keywords like "metaverse," "web3," "extended reality," and so on to receive links to news containing them every day or week. You only need to use the following URL: www.google.com/alerts.

## Watch the Market

In such a fast-paced environment as the development of the emerging Metaverse, it is imperative to watch new start-ups and investments around innovative ideas or technologies that may arise. A good practice is to check innovation projects that have been granted recently. You can check American companies or universities that received an innovation development grant (in the SBIR or STTR programs) at www.sbir.gov or do the same about European granted projects in the CORDIS database by visiting this URL: https://cordis.europa.eu.

You can also check for new serious crowdfunding initiatives performed by start-up companies that typically ask for over a million U.S. dollars in equity crowdfunding platforms like Start Engine (www .startengine.com) or SeedInvest (www.seedinvest.com). In some of them, initiatives will be only visible if you subscribe as a potential investor, which is usually free.

Another option to watch the market evolution is to attend industry events or subscribe to journals. As an engineer, I was recognized as a Senior Member of the IEEE about 10 years ago, and I enjoy receiving its journals, webinars, and conferences, some of them about the Metaverse. You could do the same by becoming a member of this or another professional association related to state-of-the-art technologies or just attend some exhibitions and events where the Metaverse is a central topic, such as the Augmented World Expo, the Metaverse Global Congress, the Immerse Global Summit, or the Augmented Enterprise Summit.

Having worked for IDC (www.idc.com) as a research analyst, I must highlight that large IT market consulting firms such as Gartner, IDC, Forrester, and others normally publish whitepapers or market studies about different topics, including the Metaverse. Although they are normally too expensive to access as an individual, maybe your organization, university, or business school has a corporate subscription that lets you read them.

Finally, remember that you can use Google Scholar (https://scholar .google.com) to look for scientific articles using "metaverse" or "web3" keywords, for instance. Although this is more appropriate, if you want to research some specific aspect of the Metaverse from a purely technical point of view, you will find some more generalist articles that condense the state of the art, provide the results of some surveys, and other interesting findings.

## Continue Learning

My final recommendation is to keep learning always. This recommendation is not limited to learning the Metaverse but to any other topic. In this book, I tried to condense a lot of knowledge, experience, and information in a limited space, with the purpose of serving as a guide and a digested source to let you learn all the relevant aspects related to the Metaverse by spending limited time.

If you want to know more, I will be more than pleased if you decide to follow me on LinkedIn or Twitter (@byantonioflores). You can also visit the website www.thejourneytometaverse.com, where I add some information about events and topics of interest related to the Metaverse.

Thank you for letting me be with you along these lines. It has been magic: we did not need to be physically in contact or virtually in the Metaverse! Anyway, I hope we can meet by any of these means soon.

# References

Alcañiz, M., E. Bigné, and J. Guixeres. July 2019. "Virtual Reality in Marketing: A Framework, Review, and Research Agenda." *Frontiers in Psychology* 10, p. 1530.

Beard, K.W. and E.M. Wolf. 2001. "Modification in the Proposed Diagnostic Criteria for Internet Addiction." *Cyberpsychology Behavior* 4, no. 3, pp. 377–383.

Chang, C.C., R.A. Grier, J. Maynard, J. Shutko, M. Blommer, R. Swaminathan, and R. Curry. 2019. "Using a Situational Awareness Display to Improve Rider Trust and Comfort With an AV Taxi." In *Proceedings of the Human Factors and Ergonomics Society Annual Meeting* 63, pp. 2083–2087. Sage CA: Los Angeles, CA: SAGE Publications.

Childs, M., H.L. Schnieders, and G. Williams. 2012. "'This Above All: To Thine Own Self Be True': Ethical Considerations and Risks in Conducting Higher Education Learning Activities in the Virtual World Second Life™." *Interactive Learning Environments* 20, no. 3, pp. 253–269.

Cuthbertson, A. 2018. "Google Admits Giving Hundreds of Firms to Your Gmail Inbox." *The Independent*.

De Back, T.T., A.M. Tinga, and M.M. Louwerse. 2021. "Learning in Immersed Collaborative Virtual Environments: Design and Implementation." *Interactive Learning Environments*, pp. 1–19.

Dehaene, S., H. Lau, and S. Kouider. 2021. "What Is Consciousness, and Could Machines Have It?" *Robotics, AI, and Humanity* pp. 43–56.

Díaz, J., C. Saldaña, and C. Ávila. 2020. "Virtual World as a Resource for Hybrid Education." *International Journal of Emerging Technologies in Learning (iJET)* 15, no. 15, pp. 94–109.

Dionisio, J.D.N. and W.G.B.R. Gilbert III. 2013. "3D Virtual Worlds and the Metaverse: Current Status and Future Possibilities." *ACM Computing Surveys* 45, no. 3, pp. 34:1–34:38.

Dogusoy, B. 2020. "Learning to Create Educational Digital Stories: Pre-School Prospective Teachers' Flipped Classroom Experiences." *Cukurova University Faculty of Education Journal* 49, no. 2, pp. 969–994

Falchuk, B., S. Loeb, and R. Neff. 2018. "The Social Metaverse: Battle for Privacy." *IEEE Technology Society Management* 37, no. 2, pp. 52–61.

Lee, L.H., T. Braud, P. Zhou, L. Wang, D. Xu, Z. Lin, A. Kumar, C. Bermejo, and P. Hui. September 2021. "All One Needs to Know about Metaverse: A Complete Survey on Technological Singularity, Virtual Ecosystem, and Research Agenda." *Journal of LATEX class files* 14, no. 8.

Lee, L.H., T. Braud, S. Hosio, and P. Hui. 2020. "Towards Augmented Reality-Driven Human-City Interaction: Current Research and Future Challenges." ArXiv, abs/2007.09207.

Leuthardt, E.C., D.W. Moran, and T.R. Mullen. 2021. "Defining Surgical Terminology and Risk for Brain Computer Interface Technologies." *Frontiers in Neuroscience* 15, no. 599549.

Leuthardt, E.C., D.W. Moran, and T.R. Mullen. 2021. "Defining Surgical Terminology and Risk for Brain Computer Interface Technologies." *Frontiers in Neuroscience* 15, p. 599549.

Mathis, F., J.H. Williamson, K. Vaniea, and M. Khamis. 2021. "Fast and Secure Authentication in Virtual Reality Using Coordinated 3D Manipulation and Pointing." *ACM Transactions on Computer-Human Interaction* 28, no. 1, pp. 1–44.

Morrow, M., J. Iorio, G. Adamson, B. Biermann, K. Dow, T. Egawa, D. Gal, A. Greenberg, J.C. Havens, S.R. Jordan, L. Joseph, C. Karasu, H. eun Kim, S. Kesselman, S. Mann, P. Mohan, L. Morgan, P. Noriega, S. Rainey, T. Richmond, S. Rizzo, F. Rossi, L. Seeto, A. Smithson, M. Stender, and M. Zuckerman. 2021. "Extended Reality in A/IS." *The IEEE Global Initiative on Ethics of Autonomous and Intelligent Systems.*

Mystakidis, S. 2022. "Metaverse." *Encyclopedia*, pp. 486–497. 2nd ed. https://doi.org/10.3390/encyclopedia2010031.

Mystakidis, S., E. Berki, and J.P. Valtanen. 2021a. "Deep and Meaningful E-Learning With Social Virtual Reality Environments in Higher Education: A Systematic Literature Review." *Applied Sciences* 11, no. 5, p. 2412.

Mystakidis, S., M. Fragkaki, and G. Filippousis. 2021b. "Ready Teacher One: Virtual and Augmented Reality Online Professional Development for K-12 School Teachers." *Computers* 10, no. 10, p. 134.

Ning, H., H. Wang, Y. Lin, W. Wang, S. Dhelim, F. Farha, and M. Daneshmand. 2021. "A Survey on Metaverse: The State-of-the-Art, Technologies, Applications, and Challenges." arXiv preprint arXiv:2111.09673.

Oddone, K. 2019. "Even Better Than the Real Thing?" Virtual Augmented Reality School Library, SCIS Connections, Education Service Australia, Melbourne, VIC, Australia, Tech. Rep., no. 110, pp. 1–15.

Park, S., K. Min, and S. Kim. 2021. "Differences in Learning of Sustainable Gameful Experiences." *Sustainability* 13, no. 16, p. 9121.

Park, S.M. and Y.G. Kim. 2022. "A Metaverse: Taxonomy, Components, Applications, and Open Challenges." IEEE Access.

Parmaxi, A. 2020. "Virtual Reality in Language Learning: A Systematic Review and Implications for Research and Practice." *Interactive learning environments*, pp. 1–13.

Ruffner, J.W., J.E. Fulbrook, and M. Foglia. September 2004. "Near-to-Eye Display Concepts for Air Traffic Controllers." *Proceedings of SPIE* 5442, pp. 120–131.

Sancar-Tokmak, H. and B. Dogusoy. 2020. "Novices' Instructional Design Problem-Solving Processes: Second Life as a Problem-Based Learning Environment." *Interactive Learning Environments*, pp. 1–14.

Stanica, I.C., F. Moldoveanu, G.P. Portelli, M.I. Dascalu, A. Moldoveanu, and M.G. Ristea. 2020. "Flexible Virtual Reality System for Neurorehabilitation and Quality of Life Improvement." *Sensors* 20, no. 21, p. 6045.

Townsdin, S. and W. Whitmer. July 2017. "Implementing Augmented Reality in Academic Libraries." *Public Services Quarterly* 13, pp. 190–199. https://doi .org/10.1080/15228959.2017.1338541.

Wen, D., Y. Yuan, and Y.X. Li. December 2013. "Artificial Societies, Computational Experiments, and Parallel Systems: An Investigation on a Computational Theory for Complex Socioeconomic Systems." *IEEE Transactions on Services Computing* 6, no. 2, pp. 177–185.

Yu, H. and M.O. Riedl. June 2012. "A Sequential Recommendation Approach for Interactive Personalized Story Generation." *Proceedings of the 11th International Conference about Automated Agents and Multiagent Systems* 1, pp. 71–78.

# About the Author

**Flores-Galea** obtained his MSc degree in Telecommunications Engineering in 2001 and his MSc in Electronics Engineering in 2003. After working as a university professor, an entrepreneur, and in some roles in large international corporations like HP, France Telecom, and NTT, he got his International Executive MBA in 2013 from IESE Business School (Spain) with part of the program attended in CEIBS (China).

Distinguished as a Senior Member of IEEE in 2012, the largest engineers' association worldwide, Flores-Galea is an active member of the "IEEE P3129 Standard for Robustness Testing and Evaluation of Artificial Intelligence-based Image Recognition Service Committee," the "IEEE P3123 Standard for Artificial Intelligence and Machine Learning Terminology and Data Formats Committee," "the IEEE European Public Policy Committee on Artificial Intelligence," and the "IEEE European Public Policy Committee for Engagement on Grid Stability." Previously, he held the position of Vice President of the IEEE Technology and Engineering Management Society for the Spanish Chapter between 2013 and 2017.

Flores-Galea has acted as a Technology Expert for the European Commission since 2019 on the subjects of AI, next-generation networks, and robotics. He has extensive experience in innovation and strategic consulting for IT and Communications topics and currently runs the Global Institute of Advisors as the CEO.

Before this book, he wrote six other ones, most of them about specific technologies explained to business roles, five scientific articles in congresses (CyberCamp, ESTYLF, Telecom I+D, FITCE, and Histelcom), and over 60 others in professional journals and magazines. He has given more than 70 keynote conferences and executive seminars to ICT leaders (C-Level suite members) during his period as a research analyst in IDC Research.

Flores-Galea has founded four start-up companies and is a member of the Board of the "Privacy and Digital Rights" journal (RDU Group), besides working as an adviser for many other organizations worldwide.

Website: www.antonioflores.eu

# Other Published Books

- "Due Diligence for Startups: a Step-by-Step Guide," Capitol Partners, 2016. ISBN: 978-1539606826.
- "Shape Memory Alloys, Muscle Wires and Robotics," Capitol Partners, 2016, ISBN: 978-1533285607.
- "Tao: traducción y contexto," Capitol Partners, 2016, ISBN: 978-1530782710 (Spanish).
- "International Trade using the Cloud," CreateSpace, 2012, ISBN: 978-1480250307.
- "50 claves para el éxito de tu empresa," Creaciones Copyright, 2011, ISBN: 978-8492779789 (Spanish).
- "BlackBerry," Creaciones Copyright, 2008, ISBN: 978-8496300712 (Spanish).

# Index

## Concise and Applied Business Books